Grace On Fire

Sherri Weeks

Copyright © 2017 Out of the Box Productions
Sherri Weeks
All rights reserved.
ISBN: 0692846379
ISBN-13: 978-0692846377

Dedication

First and foremost, thank you God for this opportunity. Your gifts are always good and I am grateful for all you have given to my family and me. I dedicate this book to you. Giving it back for you to use it for your glory and to help others in some small way find healing, hope and a closer relationship with you. I pray for the world to find your grace and love. May your grace catch fire and burn wild.
Grace on Fire!

Table of Contents

Chapter		Page
1	Tides of Grace	16
2	Sands of Grace	29
3	The Ripples of Grace	36
4	The Folds of Grace	46
5	Drops of Grace	57
6	The Wholeness of Grace	69
7	Healing Grace	80
8	The Boldness of Grace	94
9	The Circle of Grace	108
10	The Edge of Grace	124
11	Eyes of Grace	134
12	Days of Grace	150
13	Sounds of Grace	162
14	The Awakening of Grace	172
	Stories of Real Life Grace	182

Forward

There is a lot of talk about GRACE floating around these days and it really is no accident that so many people are just beginning to understand this dynamic concept. The fact is, with all the teaching, study and with our finite perception, we still are only revealing the outer layers of God's wonderful gift!

ENDORSEMENTS

"In a world of complexities in which we live, we need a renewed understanding of the Amazing, Great and Abounding Grace of God. Sherri Weeks in her book Grace On Fire shares candidly even through some crucibles of personal experience, the life lessons of God's Grace and Love. The perspectives and perceptions of the Grace of God at times may become eschewed along life's journey, thus the importance of being reminded of His continued desire to reveal Himself to us and through us. Sherri, through testimony and practical application reminds us of the expanse and depth of such great grace the Lord has offered to us through His love and sacrifice for us. This is a good study book for us all."

Dr. J. Doug Stringer
International Speaker, Founder and President of Turning Point Ministries Intl., Somebody Cares America Intl.,

*"In this powerful new book "Grace on Fire" by Sherri Weeks, you will dive deeper into Grace than ever before, learning how Grace plays a role in your life and that even when you don't see it or feel it, Grace is always there. This is a **"must read"** for anyone who struggles with doubt, fear, rejection or the uncertainty of his or her salvation!"*

Chuck Day
ICGMA (International Country Gospel Music Association) Male Vocalist of the Year, Song of the Year, Entertainer of the Year and Music Producer
Doctorate of Theology/Ordained Minister

"My husband & I have known Sherri for many years now, and she radiates kindness and joy to every person she meets. She lovingly reaches out to those around her with encouragement and love. Her latest book dealing with grace is a must read for the time we are living in when so many people are searching for acceptance and love, but are finding division and hatred. This book would be a great addition to any home group or cell group to dive into and use as a study book and will be the spark to bring light to those hidden areas of our hearts. Grace is such a foundational part of who we are becoming as believers and Sherri's book is perfect for helping believers catch "Grace on Fire"."

Selena Day
Author, Minister and Leader of World Race; Present Day Truth Ministries

"We've all felt it, rejection, abandonment and feelings of inadequacy. Sherri's heartfelt stories made me laugh, cry and rejoice in the promise of God's Grace. Sherri touches the very core of our hearts, to be loved and accepted. God's Grace has NO conditions. Sherri's writing makes me laugh, cry and look deeply into my own heart"."

Kathy Salinas
Business Owner / Entrepreneur

"This book is a true and honest bearing of Sherri's heart. It will open the hearts of her readers."

Diana Weeks
Playwright & Inducted Member of the Texas Playwriting Hall of Fame

Grace on Fire is a study book, with study questions at the end of each chapter, laid out with margins for personal notes, thoughts and nuggets of revelation as God reveals His truth to you.

This book was written to help each of us understand what grace is and what it looks like in the real world today. We have to accept grace in order to give grace.

The author speaks openly and candidly on a variety of subjects we all face. This world needs grace and if we all can truly grasp the heart of this book, grace will catch like fire and our world could change for the better.

GRACE on Fire!

Introduction

Grace: God's Love in Action!

Grace: mercy, to pardon, divine assistance,
"God's love in action toward those who cannot save themselves."

"In him we have redemption through his blood, the forgiveness of sins, in accordance with the riches of God's grace." Ephesians 1:7

Favor: An act done for someone, preference for someone, approving consideration

"For those who find me find life and receive favor from the Lord." Proverbs 8:35

GRACE is unmerited favor.
(Mercy is given to an undeserving people.)

Have you ever stopped at a fast food restaurant, placed your order and arrived at the drive through window to find more than what you originally ordered? The guy working there says…"I had extra and thought you might want it." That's Grace (Unmerited favor).

What about when you are at the grocery store and there is a long line and you have one item as to everyone else's 50? The person next in line motions for you to go ahead of him. He says, go ahead you only have a few items. That's Grace (Unmerited favor).

What about the time you messed up and made a big mistake? You thought you were going to get in trouble, lose your job or be reminded of it for the rest of your life. Wait…you didn't? You were forgiven; someone understood that we all make mistakes? You weren't judged or thrown to the wolves? That's Grace (Unmerited favor).

For it is by grace you have been saved, through faith—and this is not from yourselves, it is the gift of God— not by works, so that no one can boast. Ephesians 2:8-9

Out of his fullness we have all received grace in place of grace already given. John 1:16

However, I consider my life worth

Favor is Grace – Grace is Favor!

His Grace was Given Freely.

nothing to me; my only aim is to finish the race and complete the task the Lord Jesus has given me—the task of testifying to the good news of God's grace. Acts 20:24

...through whom we have gained access by faith into this grace in which we now stand. And we boast in the hope of the glory of God. Romans 5:2

Nevertheless, death reigned from the time of Adam to the time of Moses, even over those who did not sin by breaking a command, as did Adam, who is a pattern of the one to come. But the gift is not like the trespass. For if the many died by the trespass of the one man, how much more did God's grace and the gift that came by the grace of the one man, Jesus Christ, overflow to the many! Nor can the gift of God be compared with the result of one man's sin: The judgment followed one sin and brought condemnation, but the gift followed many trespasses and brought justification. Romans 5:14-16

God's grace was extended to Adam **AND** to the many who followed – even to us. (unmerited favor)

But by the grace of God I am what I am, and his grace to me was not without effect. No, I worked harder than all of them—yet not I, but the grace of God that was with me. 1 Corinthians 15:10

*But he said to me, "My grace is sufficient for you, for my power is made perfect in weakness." Therefore I will boast all the more gladly about my weaknesses, so that Christ's power may rest on me.
2 Corinthians 12:9*

Thank you God for your Grace!

As I look back over my life, I see God's great hand of grace (unmerited favor). As a child, I grew up without a father. He left when I was in second grade to support and live with a new wife and three children that were not his own. (To my understanding he also was a prescription drug addict.)

They were given my father's love, attention and financial support. It's hard for a young child to understand something like that. As I grew older, I came to realize that he had abandoned a wife and two children from a previous marriage prior to marrying my mother. As you can imagine, my brother and I felt abandoned, not good enough and rejected. (Probably just as

God is always near.

the other children had felt) This could have had serious repercussions in my life if I had not known my heavenly father, God, my Savior.

God taught me at an early age that He was all I needed. Still, it was tough on Father's Day or anytime there was a Father Daughter event etc. My heart was broken and it hurt. Through all of my school days, my mom worked two to three jobs just to keep a roof over our head. We always had lunch at school but not always dinner. I remember a time when only one can of soup was in the pantry. The great thing is "I had no idea that we were in lack". I never starved or missed out on any church trips, sports tournaments etc. God always provided. (Unmerited favor) Someone always donated, I worked to raise the money or scholarships were given.

I lived in what my husband now calls the "Sherri Bubble". I had no clue and was very naive. I think that was part of God's grace as well because, if I had known some things... who knows!

Mom kept us in church, sports and activities throughout school to keep us busy while she worked and tried to provide. Through the dumpster diving for furniture, to the government housing, God always made a way

Keep in me a pure heart!

when there seemed to be no way!

**His Grace was and is always sufficient!
His Grace is always on Fire and moving around us.**

1

Tides of Grace

One night I tossed and turned wide-awake (nothing unusual for me - four hours of sleep and I am good to go!) pondering writing a second book. I thought for sure it would be another poetry book like my first, Poetic Art. I have heard it has touched people's heart and moved them to action in their relationship with God and others, which is so exciting. Although, in true God fashion, it doesn't always work out the way we think it will. I kept hearing the word GRACE. Grace? Ok, I got this. I have been writing poetry and music since I was 15. I can write poems on grace, use some new art pieces etc... As I picked up a pencil to write, words began to flow as if I were writing for a retreat or a special sermon. How is this going to fit? As I wrote I saw pieces of poetic words forming

Even when we don't see it, God's hand is always moving in our lives!

beautiful visions of what God wanted to express in this book.

Therefore, you will find poetic words with vision in the beginning of each chapter. God loves to speak to me through pictures. It's the artist in me and it's how I respond back to God. There are little side notes in the margins of each page. They are "little extras" that God has spoken to me and I left room for your "special nuggets of truth" that God will give you as well.

As you will learn, I am a very open and honest person and I touch on subjects that you will not find in other Bible studies out there today. In a world full of anger and bitterness, racial fights and sexual immorality I try to find grace and love in every situation. Do you? Do you want to know how you can walk in grace like this?

I also believe that God has given us the gift of laughter therefore, you will find several true and very funny stories of my life and real life grace through it all. I am said to be very creative, a bit quirky and love to

God is always speaking!

We just have to listen.

laugh so, hold on as we laugh, cry and find truth as we study God's word and learn how to put it in action!

As I began writing this book, the first thing I asked myself "What is grace?"

What would your first response be to this question? At first I thought, grace is calm under pressure, a stability and quiet strength. Someone can be graceful in his or her presence or posture. God gives us grace to endure and grace to walk through the trials of this life etc…Well, being the good little "raised in the Baptist church" Christian that I am…I looked it up in the back of my Bible. It defines grace as God's free and unmerited favor for a sinful humanity. Webster's Dictionary defines unmerited favor as the following:

Unmerited: the opposite of a reward or deserving
Favor: an act done for someone, preference for someone, approving consideration

So let's dive in and take a look at what God has shared with us about His grace and how to apply it in our everyday lives.

His grace is sufficient. It is enough! We cannot understand the depths of His love & grace.

<u>(Here are some of the poetic words forming a vision…)</u>

They roll, rumble and press toward the shore. At their peak they foam and become white. The dark color of their underbelly reveals the churning up of all the dirt and impurities that lie beneath. As they quiet and hit the shore their temperament turns to peace. The raging has ended only to subside and return again. Out to sea…movement begins. Who knows the depths in which it all begins but our eyes see way before the horizon. This is the ebb and flow of the ocean.

Our lives mimic the ebb and flow of the tide…times of stillness, times of rage, movement forward and times of peace. I find that even in the stillness there is movement, things undetectable to the human eye or conceivable to the human mind.

This is when grace is on fire.

God is in control, no matter what evil is around us!

Grace going before us, moving behind us and all alongside of us…I look back at times of unrest and see the footprint of grace (God, alongside of me). His grace has carried me, sustained me and it holds me every hour of every day. (Even when I am not consciously aware)

…to the praise of His glorious grace, which He has freely given us in the one He loves. In Him we have redemption through His blood, the forgiveness of sins, in accordance with the riches of God's grace. That He lavished on us with all wisdom and understanding.
Ephesians 1:6- 8

When you have done all you can do… just STAND!

There are moments in life where your life is so unraveled there seems to be no way that it could ever be restored. Our family has journeyed through many of those times but the most vivid memory is when we had the police standing at our door late at night. Our middle school son had been accused of something that was not even a buzzword or spoken about in our home. We could not imagine a child of that age even knowing what it was, much less doing it. The enemy was playing a tough game.

Earlier, my son had been playing hide and seek with neighbors. One child accused him of trying to "take advantage" of her physically. (So let's call it like it was…. she accused him of touching her inappropriately and trying to assault her - rape) WHAT? Are you kidding me? That was pretty much my first response. I didn't even know what it meant until college…Seriously! (Sherri bubble) The only thing I remember the police saying after that was jail. Charges were never filed and the girl denied any testing. Later, we found out that her sister had been in that situation so; it was definitely a buzzword in their home. I am sure her parents only wanted to protect both daughters, which I would as well.

I was numb at the thought of my son being sent to jail for years for something in which I knew he was innocent. We all looked like deer in the headlights. (No clue what was happening) After speaking with our son we realized he had only asked her for a "smooch". She said no and went home. (Innocent kids stuff...)

After speaking with the police, I walked to the neighbors, tears streaming down my face and trembling. I pleaded with them, parent to parent to drop the charges, imagine your middle school child going to jail?" I pleaded and pleaded, "Please don't take my child". I was still convinced he had done nothing majorly wrong. I thought I was going to die right there when they took their daughters side and closed the door.

The next three weeks were...well, honestly I don't remember much other than it was the only thing I could think of every moment of every day. I had prayed the first night or so..."please God save my son" and then I didn't know what to pray. I just STOOD in faith knowing that

You CAN have Break-through!

somehow God would turn this around for my son's good and God's glory.

The call finally came, the judge dismissed the case and the young girl confessed of the lie! Wow! "Really?" What a relief. My heart was full of gratitude and thankfulness to my God. I questioned, "Why did we have to go through this?" Peace finally came and **God's grace covered us!**

Have you ever been in a place where your strength wasn't enough? Your understanding of a situation wasn't there? Did you want to give up? Give in? We have all been there, that's when God's grace steps in. His grace, peace and love can give you all you need – but it comes with a catch. **You have to accept it!** Knowing and believing the God of the Universe, the King of Kings stepped down from heaven, became man, gave himself just for you. Yes – **you were worth it** – He rose again and waits for you to invite Him in.

For it is by grace you have been saved, through faith, and this is not from yourselves, it is the gift of God,

> **No matter what our background or how hard we try to live good and moral lives. We cannot earn salvation or remove our sin**

not by works, so that no one can boast. Ephesians 2:8-9

Jesus answered, "I am the way and the truth and the life. No one comes to the Father except through me. John 14:6

If you declare with your mouth, "Jesus is Lord," and believe in your heart that God raised him from the dead, you will be saved. Romans 10:9

For it is with your heart that you believe and are justified, and it is with your mouth that you profess your faith and are saved. Romans 10:10

Prayer of Salvation:
God, I can't imagine going through life any longer without you. I want to have your grace and love in my life. I may not fully understand what Sherri is talking about but I want to know

the peace and grace that she has experienced in her life. I believe that you are who you say you are. You sent your son to die for me and on the third day rose again. I know that my life has been full of sin and I do not deserve to be saved but I understand enough to know that your grace covers me and your love captures me. Please forgive me of all my sins and take me in as your child. I give you all of my life and my heart. Come in and make a home in me. Fill me with your Spirit and lead me in the path of righteousness. I am yours and you are mine. Thank you for loving me enough to save me. I love you daddy God. In Jesus name. Amen!

If you have done this and truly accepted Him as your Savior– you are His child. God's favorite, the child with unmerited favor! (His grace)

We cannot save ourselves. Christ died to save us from our sins.

There is nothing you can do or have done to earn this grace. **He just loves you that much!** Believing is Living and Living is Believing.

Making your choice to follow and obey God means that you have been given the opportunity to apply God's grace as you walk through hard times in your life. We do not always feel like obeying and sometimes we let hurts get in the way of loving the way God wants us to love. God's grace is powerful and when we cry out for God's help in times of trouble He is faithful to meet us right where we are in our life. Your life will not be perfect; neither will you so, let yourself off the hook right now. Connect with a strong Bible teaching and Spirit lead church or group to continue your growth.

I am a child of God!

Welcome Home!

Your life will now be forever changed for good!

Chapter Questions:

1. What truth is in your heart when you are hurting or going through a difficult time in your life?

2. Do you cry out for God's grace? Or do you go to the "phone before the throne"? (i.e.: call a friend and whine first)

3. Is God allowing the circumstances in your life to be less than perfect to show you the command of truth in your heart?

4. What is your normal response to the trials in your life? Do you accept and apply God's grace during these times?

2

Sands of Grace

Do I really know what grace is? How do I live with grace?

Like the tiny grains of sand that fills an hourglass and the beaches within our soul, God's grace is as endless.

Each one should use whatever gift he has received to serve others, faithfully administering God's grace in its various forms. I Peter 4:10

As I walk along the beach I look closely to see the tiny particles of sand and I realize God's grace is like those particles. Millions upon millions combined together give us a sure footing, a strong foundation in which to walk. Can you imagine trying to walk in quick sand? It's not the same. Quick sand will pull you down, cause you to sink and even die - without grace that would be our future, our demise.

    I am so thankful for God's grace

and His mercy and He chose to give it to me. (In spite of my flaws, sins and unworthiness) What grace has been given that I may walk on sand without sinking?

For grace is my foothold!

As I continue to walk, I see the purity of the sand close to the water and the further I walk away, I begin to see weeds and unclean places within the dunes. The white sand becomes dark and shady. What a great picture. God's word says that He is life-giving water (a spring of living water). The ocean is a picture of that water. He purifies those who draw near. If we continually walk away or keep our distance, then weeds and pollutants begin to invade our lives.

Lord, you are the hope of Israel; all who forsake you will be put to shame. Those who turn away from you will be written in the dust because they have forsaken the Lord, the spring of living water.
Jeremiah 17:13

We are FREE in Christ!

Whoever believes in me, as Scripture has said, rivers of living water will flow from within them. John 7:38

See to it that no one misses the grace of God and that no bitter root grows up to cause trouble and defile many. Hebrews 12:15

As I walk and examine my heart, I see where weeds have taken root and bitterness has invaded. I am undone in His presence! My face in the sand brings tears to my eyes and a puddle begins to form. In the middle of a public beach is usually not my ideal spot for heart surgery but when God moves, we have to allow Him to do whatever needs to be done. He wants to tear down and uproot all of the issues that have brought me to this place. He must tear down to build up! It's still our choice to allow Him to do heart surgery.

When we allow God to tear down our strongholds / issues we will receive His promises and blessings. We have to plant God's truth in our heart so He can uproot the things that

Having a good foundation is important.

cause us to stumble and make bad choices. **We all need a heart transplant!** God is sovereign and He sees all of our desires, motivations, thoughts, intentions etc. He knows the condition of your heart.

But the Lord said to Samuel, "Do not consider his appearance or his height, for I have rejected him. The Lord does not look at the things people look at. People look at the outward appearance, but the Lord looks at the heart." 1 Samuel 16:7

I will give you a new heart and put a new spirit in you; I will remove from you your heart of stone and give you a heart of flesh. And I will put my Spirit in you and move you to follow my decrees and be careful to keep my laws. Ezekiel 36:26-27

Never add to or twist God's truth.

There have been times when I think my heart is like glass or tiny particles of sand dripping through the hands of my father. Many times I have let the root of rejection "set up shop" and when touched, it brings me to my knees. I have allowed others comments, behaviors, brokenness etc. water my own heart. And let me tell you, when two people have the root of rejection taking up residence in their heart, it can become very painful, very quickly. The biggest thing that I have learned is not to let others water my heart, no matter how good their intentions. God and His truths are the water and nourishment for our healing. His grace covers our rooted heart and us.

> Think Before You Speak!

His grace is enough!

Chapter Questions

1. Are you going through something that makes you feel like you're standing in quick sand about to go under? Stop and let God take that burden and heal your heart.

2. What are some areas in which you feel need uprooting in your heart?

> Whatever is in my heart and mind will find a way out!

3. Have you ever allowed God to do heart surgery? If not, open your heart to healing and allow Him to take away pain from the past.

4. In what ways will you plant God's word in your heart to replace the bad seeds that have been uprooted? Make a plan and stay with it.

> Think positive...no "stinkin thinkin"

3

Ripples of Grace

The hues of green ripple in the wind within a backdrop of splendor, while the mountains beckon His worship... Majestic they stand calling out to their creator. Take a deep breath in God's grace in nature. One rustle of a leaf, one ray of light on the hills, one distant song and the gentle breeze... all ripples that come surging toward me, filling me and bringing me into His presence. Throw a stone into the water and see the ripples of its effect. The water cannot stay still from the plunging stone. It's weight too great that the water has no choice but to be affected. Beauty in motion, cause and effect. Without hesitation it moves, it bends and changes it's form.

Change is good!

For I know the plans I have for you," declares the Lord, "plans to prosper you and not to harm you, plans to give you hope and a future. Then you will call on me and come and pray to me, and I will listen to you. You will seek me and find me when you seek me with all your heart. Jeremiah 29:11-13

> **Live a Life of Worship!**

Most days we hate the word change. Don't we? In order to grow, we must change. As we allow God to uproot our heart, there will be change. You are no longer the same. Our heart is where our beliefs and truths are stored. They are based on past experiences whether true or not we have bought into lies. Some lies that we have bought into might be:

I'm ugly – I'm fat – I'm not loveable – I'm stupid – I'm not worthy – I'm rejected – No one likes me etc.

> **God does not create JUNK. He created you in His image!**

These things can play like videotape in our mind over and over. Sometimes when we hear something enough, we begin to believe it. (True or not) At this point, we can hear God's word and truth but until we remove the lies from our heart we will never truly believe it. His word must be hidden in our heart!

I have hidden your word in my heart that I might not sin against you.
Psalm 119:11

God wants the condition of our heart to be fertile (good soil to plant new seed – new truths – His truths). In order for this to happen He has to uproot the lies. So what does your heart look like? Is it soft, broken, ready to receive? God tells us not to let our hearts be hardened. We must have our hearts softened toward God so that His truths can penetrate and infiltrate the rough, rocky and hard places.

My sacrifice, O God, is a broken spirit; a broken and contrite heart you, God, will not despise.
Psalm 51:17

I know a big root I have dealt with is

God is always truthful, fair and just.

trust. (More like-distrust) I have had people use me my entire life. (Most of the time without even knowing it - Sherri bubble) As an adult, I have had many of those moments. Therefore, even as a mature and strong believer, I don't trust people very often. I tend to keep my distance until I truly know it is safe. I guess I'm a little "gun shy". I would love for everyone in the world to be people of their word and be "what you see is what you get" kind of people. I want people to be the "real deal", loving, kind, always making an effort to love and befriend someone. Unfortunately, it doesn't work that way. I know....idealistic. People are people and we all have faults. High (over the top) expectations can get us into trouble and hurt. (Been there, done that and got the t-shirt!)

Therefore, when we establish our truth in our heart it creates hardness, doubt, unbelief, thorns, rocks and dryness. God never meant for this. When we go through painful experiences and we know God's truth, we can apply faith, God's strength and

> **It is useless to blame anyone else for our sin. We must answer to Him for how we live.**

His grace to get us through it. His truth will produce peace, righteousness, joy and love!

During tough situations, especially those we have experienced before, our response can be to flee, hide, protect ourselves, explode in anger etc. There may even be places where we have decided, "these are off limits"; places where you do not want God to see, touch or heal. Maybe it's too familiar? What would you do without it? It's all you know… You wear it almost like a badge of honor.

For this people's heart has become calloused; they hardly hear with their ears, and they have closed their eyes. Otherwise they might see with their eyes, hear with their ears, understand with their hearts and turn, and I would heal them. Matthew 13:15

Let's get rid of the hardness and callousness of our heart. We have been deceived, causing unbelief, distrust and doubt. This only makes us deaf, blind and lame. We cannot hear, see or walk in the healing God is offering until we allow Him and His truths to penetrate our heart.

The wisdom of the prudent is to give thought to their ways, but the folly of fools is deception. Proverbs 14:8

We must allow God to work in our lives…Just give up now; it's the best way and saves you so much heartache down the road! He's going to do it anyway so let him use the circumstances in your life to produce righteousness and healing.
    Let Him apply His grace!

> **We are accountable to God before anyone else!**

Consider it pure joy, my brothers and sisters, whenever you face trials of many kinds, because you know that the testing of your faith produces perseverance. Let perseverance finish its work so that you may be mature and complete, not lacking anything. James 1:2-4

He loves you so much that he does not want you to live with these lies and produce bad fruit. He wants to break up the hard and fallow ground in your heart to bring good soil and plant seeds of truth, righteousness, peace, love and grace.

**His amazing grace!
His grace is amazing!**

God's love is never-ending.

Chapter Questions

1. What do you think of change? Does it scare you? Are you open to it? Have you been through change lately?

2. What videotape plays in your mind over and over? What words have you spoken or believed about yourself?

3. What one root has taken up residence in your heart that you know is a struggle or going to be tough to get rid of?

4. Do you believe that God can heal you and uproot this issue to bring you into a place of healing? If not, why? (What other root keeps you from receiving God's grace and healing)

Change
can be
good.

Sow righteousness for yourselves, reap the fruit of unfailing love, and break up your unplowed ground; for it is time to seek the Lord, until he comes and showers his righteousness on you.
Hosea 10:12

4

The Folds of Grace

Within the folds of His love we find grace – grace to cover and carry us.

Strengthen the feeble hands, steady the knees that give way; say to those with fearful hearts, "Be strong, do not fear; your God will come, he will come with vengeance; with divine retribution he will come to save you. Then will the eyes of the blind be opened and ears of the deaf unstopped. Then will the lame leap like a deer, and the mute tongue shout for joy. Water will gush forth in the wilderness and streams in the desert. The burning sand will become a pool, the thirsty ground bubbling springs. In the haunts where jackals once lay, grass and reeds and papyrus will grow.
Isaiah 35:3-7

Lying bare and open on the branch, he quietly moves underneath to begin his journey. Within the grace God has given he finds what he needs to spin and turn forming a dense white cocoon. The incubation process has begun and a deep sleep falls upon him as he is enveloped within the denseness of his existence. The quiet is deafening, as he lay lifeless among the vastness of his environment. The light trickles in between the folds of thinly woven strands. He is folded up in protection while changing into his new form. The time has come for his new life to begin. There is life; there is movement beneath the white cocoon. One piercing blow brings forth this new life. A wing appears and then another... The cocoon opens up to reveal the beauty that has transformed within the walls of security. He waits; He adjusts and flies!

The new has begun and his perspective has changed!

I think we all have been there, when

> **The process of maturing in our faith takes time.**

strongholds and hurts get the best of us. I know I have wanted to climb in my own cocoon and start again many times. I remember growing up having a strong urge to perform. I began singing at the age of 2 and never stopped. Early on, I realized I could get approval and acceptance from my good performance, whether it was on the stage, on the field, in the classroom or being the "perfect child". (Whatever that meant) There was much expectation placed on me growing up (whether it was from others or myself). I felt like a failure if I was not perfect or do the expected.

Now remember, I was naive, so I really had no clue this was going on in my life. This was the condition of my heart. Plus, I thought if I were perfect, then no one else I cared about would leave or abandon me. (I know.... crazy but that's what I thought) Therefore, my expectations of myself were extremely high and at times unreasonable and unattainable.

I never put that kind of pressure on others as I did myself. When I did not reach my goals or be who I thought I should be at the time…self-hatred came in to play. Let's just say low self-esteem was my closest friend although; on the outside I looked like I had it all together. I took this one with me into adulthood and finally allowed God to heal me. (The struggle still pops up its ugly head now and then) I could have taken the wrong road many times but…by the grace of God! I have changed and continue to change as I walk this road called life. (Sometimes I am still in the "Sherri bubble")

What is a stronghold?
- A snare or a pitfall
- Betrayed or taken unaware
- Deception
- Holding back

A trap seizes him by the heel; a snare holds him fast. A noose is hidden for him on the ground; a trap lies in his path. Terrors startle him on every side and dog his every step. Calamity is hungry for him; disaster is ready for him when he falls. Job 18:9-12

Wow, I think of Job and all of his struggles. (Talk about a snare and

Just ASK!

trap) The enemy of our soul (Satan) wants to entrap us, cause us to miss the mark and call of God's purpose for our lives. He wants us to rebel against God. He is always lurking around trying to stir up trouble. He wants us to have unforgiveness and judgments that form walls around our heart. He will use people in our life, whether believer or nonbeliever, to build up callouses in our heart. He also can use television, movies, video games, music etc.… as well to hinder our walk with God.

Strongholds can also be from wrong beliefs, opinions or traditions passed down from our parents or from someone of influence in our lives. They can capture our mind. Repenting is the key. Repent from the generational curse(s) passed down on you and pray for the generations to come. Pray for these strongholds not to be a snare to those who follow.

God's grace is sufficient and His mercies are new every morning!

Be alert and of sober mind. Your enemy the devil prowls around like a roaring lion looking for someone to devour. I Peter 5:8

The thief comes only to steal and kill and destroy; I have come that they may have life, and have it to the full. John 10:10

Do not allow the enemy a place in your thinking or your heart. We must obey God's commands and truths. If we hold on to God's truths, the enemy cannot keep us in bondage. We can be enfolded in God's grace and freedom.

Blessed is the one who perseveres under trial because, having stood the test, that person will receive the crown of life that the Lord has promised to those who love him. When tempted, no one should say, "God is tempting me." For God cannot be tempted by evil, nor does he tempt anyone; but each person is tempted when they are dragged away by their own evil desire and enticed. Then, after desire has conceived, it

> It is in the abandonment of our strength and our will that we can find a place of complete trust in His care!

gives birth to sin; and sin, when it is full-grown, gives birth to death.
James 1:12-15

It is in the abandonment of our strength and our will where we can find a place of complete trust and in His care. Deliverance is found in the name of the Lord. Freedom is found in Christ and Christ alone.

If my people, who are called by my name, will humble themselves and pray and seek my face and turn from their wicked ways, then I will hear from heaven, and I will forgive their sin and will heal their land.
2 Chronicles 7:14

The weapons we fight with are not the weapons of the world. On the contrary, they have divine power to demolish strongholds. We demolish arguments and every pretension that sets itself up against the knowledge of God, and we take captive every thought to make it obedient to Christ. And we will be ready to punish every act of disobedience, once your obedience is complete.

2 Corinthians 10:4-6

You belong to your father, the devil, and you want to carry out your father's desires. He was a murderer from the beginning, not holding to the truth, for there is no truth in him. When he lies, he speaks his native language, for he is a liar and the father of lies.   John 8:44

God will give us a strategy to tear down strongholds, even in the places we think cannot change. He says...."I AM able!"

Praise be to the Lord, who has not let us be torn by their teeth. We have escaped like a bird from the fowler's snare; the snare has been broken, and we have escaped. Our help is in the name of the Lord, the Maker of heaven and earth.
Psalm 124:6-8

He Is Able!

Chapter Questions

1. Do you have a memory from your youth that brings a stronghold to mind? How did it take root in your heart?

2. Did your parent's views or opinion shape your views and opinions in any way? What and how?

3. What stronghold is keeping you from moving forward? Is there anything that keeps popping up?

4. God wants you to release that stronghold and to hear you say…"take it, it's yours". Will you do that today?

Let's Pray:

Lord, I have let this take a hold of my life for way too long. I want to be free from _____. This is no longer a part of who I am and I release _____ into your hands. I ask that as you take it from my heart, you fill the space with your love, peace, forgiveness and grace. I know it is more than a feeling and there will be times where the enemy wants to bring it up again but I will choose to run to you. I will not let it control my life and I will remember it was given to you freely and you have taken care of it. Thank you for being my daddy God. You take away my sin and replace it with your truth. I love you and I choose to walk in freedom and forgiveness. In Jesus' name. Amen!

Help me to
forgive as
you have
forgiven
me.

5

Drops of Grace

Rushing waters or drops of dew, we can seethe precipitation that has gathered from the unseen. We did not see the rushing river form or gather water within its banks. We did not see any precipitation causing the early morning dew to rest on the blades of grass but we see the residue or the "after effect" of something.

There are times in my life when I see God's hand rushing in like a mighty river and at times it drops like dew in small amounts when I need it most. (Sometimes when I did not realize I needed it) I have come to a place in my life where I accept the things I cannot change and I ask for the Grace to change the things I do have control over. (Easier said then done, I know.)

I have noticed as I go throughout

my day I need those drops of grace along the way. My temper runs short when a car cuts in front of me almost causing a wreck. I find no patience waiting in a "15 item limit" line at the store and see a woman checking out who has 50 items and the clerk still lets her go through the line. Things like this happen and they tend to happen all in the same day! Right? For instance, kids spreading peanut butter all over your floors and walls, the dishwasher breaks and your plumbing is backed up. Have you been there? Boy, do I need those drops of grace through those days!

*That's when **Grace is on Fire** and those drops come pouring in; if we stay aware and awake to see and receive them, we will be blessed and we will grow in grace!*

Ever felt like you're just walking around aimlessly through life? Have you ever felt betrayed? Have you gone through a divorce or ugly break up with a friend? Have you been knocked down and struggled to get up? Have you lost your way? We have all been there. You are not down for the count but the enemy of your soul would have you believe otherwise.

Consider it pure joy, my brothers and sisters, whenever you face trials of many kinds, because you know that the testing of your faith produces perseverance. Let perseverance finish its work so that you may be mature and complete, not lacking anything. James 1:2 -4

The righteous cry out, and the Lord hears them; he delivers them from all their troubles. Psalm 34:17

No matter what your situation, and we all have them…. don't give up, keep coming back and keep getting up no matter how many times you are knocked down. We cannot let pride or obstinance get in our way.

> *"Our obstinance will make us obsolete." Beth Moore*
> *"Yielding is ineffective."*
> *Sherri Weeks (lol)*

Why are we content with blending in when we were created to stand out?

"Resistance is futile." **The Borg (just for Star Trek fans...lol)**

God wants us all to make a difference in this world. We cannot make a difference if we are not willing to change or allow God to move within us. We do not want to become stagnant...it reminds me of stagnant water that has no ebb and flow...no movement whatsoever. You know, it has green algae and slime on top. I don't think there is much use for slimy, stagnant water.

We can get comfortable with our lives and we don't always want change - do we? We like having things the same and doing things the same way we have always done them - right? But, there are times when God wants to bring change. He knows where He wants to move us. Sometimes, He has to drop a grenade in the middle of it to make us move out of the old and into the new.

As we move forward we must take our focus off what we think we are loosing and focus on what we are gaining!

Grace is on Fire within God ordained change!

Now, BREATHE: (No really…take a deep breathe)
He is in the deep and the shallow breaths within our lives!
(I love how God gave this saying to Beth Moore and gave it to me shortly before doing one of her studies…God knows how to reach us!)

The Spirit of God has made me; the breath of the Almighty gives me life. Job 33:4

"A time is coming and in fact has come when you will be scattered, each to your own home. You will leave me all alone. Yet I am not alone, for my Father is with me." John 16:32

Be strong and courageous. Do not be afraid or terrified because of them, for the Lord your God goes with you; he will never leave you nor forsake you." Deuteronomy 31:6

FAITH is a verb!

Remember, you are not alone even in the change. But let me say…if your life or situations have not changed in 15 years…there's something wrong. We all should be moving up and forward bearing fruit for God's glory!

So, what do we do when God brings change?

First, we have to accept with change God will make a way when there seems to be no way and He has a plan. He will always turn it for our good and for His glory.

For I know the plans I have for you," declares the Lord, "plans to prosper you and not to harm you, plans to give you hope and a future. Jeremiah 29:11

And we know that in all things God works for the good of those who love him, who have been called according to his purpose. Romans 8:28

Second, sometimes we need a little guidance or mentoring because no one

> Growth is essential – It begins with faith and culminates in love for

has all the answers. We are all in need of mentors and leaders who will inspire and teach us God's Word and how to walk it out in the real world.

Do you have anyone that you mentor? Is there anyone in your life that is always there for you? We have to be careful not to let mentors become idols. It's all about balance. As a child our parents have the greatest influence in our lives (just as you do if you are a parent) and it affects our views in all areas of life and how we view ourselves.

I recently took a Beth Moore Bible Study. She taught that we could become unbalanced and accept only the maternal (mother) or the paternal (father) correction and influence in our life. I was curious to see how I would line up since I grew up in a single parent home. Let's look at some qualities we might have and see if we line up on one side or the other. (I have added some of my own thoughts on each.)

Maternal: (If we have too much mothering)

We **can** become Soft
We **can** be Self-Indulgent
We **can** be Self-Excusing
We **can** be Hyper Sensitive
We **can** be Narcissistic (It's all about us)
We **can** be Self-Fulfilling needs
You **can** "grace" yourself out of obedience

Paternal: **(If we have too much fathering)**
We **can** be overly realistic
We **can** have a Harder Heart
We **can** be Performance Driven
We **can** be Become over – over achievers
We **can** be Critical and Judgmental
We **can** be forget to give grace to others

> Any missing piece – is missing peace.

As the oldest child in our single parent home, I had some major responsibilities. Mom worked three jobs to put food on the table and left me in charge many times. As I reflected over this list, I had some tendencies from the maternal and paternal side. I was soft and overly sensitive but I also was performance driven and an over achiever at times.

But, I have learned through it all - it is so wonderful to have the love of your mom. One who is all in, totally committed and loves you no matter what and can no longer chase you down! It makes life so peaceful. LOL

I'm just kidding…she never chased me down too much. Although, I still needed work going into my adulthood. So, when we take these attributes into account we have to know God wants to heal us and bring us into complete wholeness.

We are like puzzles yet to be completed and when the puzzle is complete (so, we think) there are pieces still missing. God is the missing pieces! He is the only one that can complete us and make us whole.

I love this saying: Any missing piece is missing peace!

No matter what our background or how hard we try to live good and moral lives, we cannot earn salvation or remove our sin.

> *For it is by grace you have been saved, through faith—and this is not from yourselves, it is the gift of God— not by works, so that no one can boast.* *Ephesians 2:8-9*

At some point we have to believe this in our heart.

Chapter Questions

1. Do you feel like you are aimlessly walking through life? (Explain what's going on. You have to acknowledge it before you can address it.)

2. What kind of changes do you want to make in your life? Has God already begun to bring change for you? How do you feel about that change?

God can work through any opposition.

3. Did you grow up with a single mom or dad? Did you have a stronger influence in your life more so than the other? (maternal or paternal)

4. List some of the tendencies you can relate to or see in your self within this list. Ask God to bring His grace into every situation and to bring balance and healing in those tendencies.

6

The Wholeness of Grace

> We are made whole through grace

To be whole: comprising of the full quantity, amount, extent, containing all the elements, properly belonging; complete: not broken, damaged, or impaired.

I love the last definition: complete, not broken or impaired. What a great picture of wholeness! I truly believe that is God's plan for all of us but we will not be perfect and may not see the fullness of perfection here on earth. We can however, find the wholeness His grace offers and be the best us we can be.

Here is a picture of wholeness:
Finally, be strong in the Lord and in his mighty power. Put on the full armor of God, so that you can take your stand against the devil's

schemes. For our struggle is not against flesh and blood, but against the rulers, against the authorities, against the powers of this dark world and against the spiritual forces of evil in the heavenly realms. Therefore put on the full armor of God, so that when the day of evil comes, you may be able to stand your ground, and after you have done everything, to stand. Stand firm then, with the belt of truth buckled around your waist, with the breastplate of righteousness in place, and with your feet fitted with the readiness that comes from the gospel of peace. In addition to all this, take up the shield of faith, with which you can extinguish all the flaming arrows of the evil one. Take the helmet of salvation and the sword of the Spirit, which is the word of God. And pray in the Spirit on all occasions with all kinds of prayers and requests. With this in mind, be alert and always keep on praying for all the Lord's people.
Ephesians 6:10-18

Helmet of Salvation means…
You are desired and loved
He went to great lengths to show His love for you
Your Parental Relationship is balanced
You are wanted by God
He is waiting for you to make note of His presence
He loved you first and delights in you
God has given you a renewed mind
He has saved you from a life of death
You are living life more abundantly

Breastplate of Righteousness means…
You are nurtured and you welcome Him to nurture you
You are His "little girl / boy"
He protects you with His righteous hand
It Guards Your Heart
He exhorts (instructs) and encourages (inspires) you
You stand up for what's right and true in the eyes of the Lord
You do not give up or back down (do not shrink back)

Sword of the Spirit means...
You Study the Word of God
You live a life of prayer - Praying at all times
You know that you are built on the Rock
You take Him at His word -God Breathed and inspired
You speak the Word of God in power and truth

Shield of Faith means...
It quenches the fiery darts of the enemy
You Believe
You live a life without fear & knowing that He will do what He says He will do
You extend grace – which believes His promises & delivers us
You are living an undiscouraged & undefeated life

Belt of Truth means...
When you accept Jesus Christ as Savior, He pours himself into you
He holds you accountable
You're the dwelling of His spirit (He

Walk in truth with love

loves you from the inside out)
You know who you are & Love yourself according to His truth
You know what you are purposed to do

Shoes of Peace means…
You are walking worthy
You are doing what He has called you to do
Your speech & actions reflect your sanctification
You do not stir up dissention
You love others – without measure
You accept who He is and who you are in Christ

(*Some excerpts taken from Beth Moore's study – Children of the day)

This is a picture of a secure and whole child of God. Most of us are missing pieces. If you really look and study each of these you may find some of your deepest insecurities. Insecurities that God wants to heal. Healing begins with grace.

His Grace is setting Fire to our insecurities!

So how do we find healing and peace?

1. **Ask God** for healing and repent for the places where we have allowed someone else to be an idol in our lives. We must connect to the source (God).

Peter replied, "Repent and be baptized, every one of you, in the name of Jesus Christ for the forgiveness of your sins. And you will receive the gift of the Holy Spirit. Acts 2:38

Know Jesus, Know Peace... No Jesus, No Peace

2. **Read His Word:** All the directions needed for life can be found in His word. It is nourishment for our souls.
   Know Jesus; Know peace – No Jesus, No peace!

It is to be with him, and he is to read it all the days of his life so that he may learn to revere the Lord his God and follow carefully all the words of this law and these decrees. Deuteronomy 17:19

3. **Have accountability and community:**

Be completely humble and gentle; be patient, bearing with one another in love. Ephesians 4:2

> We cannot mentor or have mentors if we separate ourselves from people. The body needs what you have and you need what they have.

As iron sharpens iron, so one person sharpens another. Proverbs 27:17

But… we have to have the right heart. We should do everything out of love! We never want to do anything because it makes us look like "good Christians." This is pride and self-serving.

He is the one we proclaim, admonishing and teaching everyone with all wisdom, so that we may present everyone fully mature in Christ. Colossians 1:28

Pride goes before destruction, a haughty spirit before a fall. Proverbs 16:18

When pride comes, then comes disgrace, but with humility comes wisdom. Proverbs 11:2

Love must be sincere. Hate what is evil; cling to what is good. Be devoted to one another in love. Honor one another above yourselves. Romans 12:9-10

We should do everything to please God & to encourage others. The command to encourage others is found throughout the Bible. In *1Thes. 5:11-23* there are several.

- 5:11 Build each other up
- 5:12 Respect leaders
- 5:13 Hold leaders in high regard and live in peace
- 5:14 Warn the idle

Hopefully, you have or can find a church or home group of like-mindedness, building relationships and growing in Christ together. It is very important to surround yourself with truth and love.

Not giving up meeting together, as some are in the habit of doing, but encouraging one another—and all the more as you see the Day approaching. Hebrews 10:25

Chapter Questions

1. Look at the Armor of God again; in what areas are you missing pieces?

2. Are there places in your heart where you have allowed idols or others to influence your life in a negative way?

3. Ask God to take away any idols and bring His truth and wholeness into your life. Give any missing pieces back to God and let Him take care of them. (Repent and release control)

4. Are you an encourager? (Not incorrigible… meaning willful, a person of their own tendencies, without correction or unruly) Set your heart and mind in the right place to be a person that encourages and loves others unconditionally. In what ways do you encourage others? What are some new ways that you might encourage someone?

> Do I influence or am I influenced?

7

Healing Grace

A look, a glance, a touch is all it takes to feel the love of someone dear. I hear the softness of the notes coming together in harmony to form a melodic tune. It reaches my soul and touches my heart with every beat. It weaves and moves in and out of time like two dancing as one but each with a distinctive sound. Music can move us all to a place of joy, reflection or deep appreciation.

Grace is like a song that moves you in the deep places of your heart. It touches you and moves you like no other. Grace brings healing. It lights a fire within us all when needed most.

Be Open to Hear and Listen

As little children we want things our way and if catered to, we grow into adults thinking we should get everything we want and do whatever we want. I have been there. There are times when we think we have paid our dues and someone owes us something or we should be able to do_____. (Fill in the blank)

Grace understands where we are right now and loves us anyway. God is so good. We have to know grace may be extended but we cannot stay in the place where we are for long. We must find healing and allow correction in order to grow and become who God intended us to be.

Grace kicks in and lights a fire!

Let me share an example of doing things your own way, refusing to be corrected or using wisdom. (It almost got me into trouble) Before children, I had a friend (well, hopefully I still have friends…) who sang in his college choir touring in the Houston area. I really wanted to go and no one was going to stop me. I had decided I was going to hop in my new little sport car and drive down to the 5th Ward by myself at night. Now, I had no idea what the 5th Ward was, I just knew I had to get there. My husband, being a native Houstonian was freaking out. He kept telling me not to go but…. willfully I refused to listen. Therefore, he had no choice but to join me in this adventure.

So, at 4pm on a Friday night (while it was still light outside) we headed on our way. We arrived at a small church where the only thing as white as were was the color of the walls. Of course, I still had no clue because my best friend was singing and color never meant anything to me. We sat down on the 5th row and right in front of us sat a little boy no older than 5 or 6. I don't think he had ever seen a white person in church before because he turned around and starred at us the entire time. His mom kept trying to get him to turn around…she would say: "turn around, it's rude to stare…" It was hysterical. We played a lot of "peek – a - boo" during the service.

If you have never been to an all black church service…let me tell you it is awesome. We had so much fun. We stood and clapped our hands and they were so passionate. They also did not have a time limit.... we did not get out of there until midnight! So, as we were trying to find our way back to the freeway, in and out of streets (yes, we got lost)...finally we saw it...the entrance ramp to the freeway. We proceeded to get over when all of the sudden.... red and blue lights!

Yes, we were pulled over just as we were making our get away! (at least that is what they thought) Two large police officers got out and surround our car on both sides. They started questioning and interrogating us like crazy. (We were definitely harassed)

They asked, "why are you down here at this time of night...selling drugs?" We have a car with your same description spotted selling drugs around here...."

We kept telling them, we were at church! Really... (sure...white people at church in the 5th Ward at midnight: for those who do not know what the 5th ward is....it is a very dangerous area at night, so I am told) They were not buying it. They began searching our car and finally saw the

When we feel powerless God can help!

church flyer on the floorboard. All of the sudden they changed their tune and said, "Have a nice night", got in their squad car and left.

It was the scariest and funniest thing ever. So, see if I would have listened…. I tend to get myself in all kinds of pickles sometimes, just by being hard headed. (I maybe a bit naive as well) I want to be perfectly clear…I do not see color. I believe people are people and all are created equal and in God's image. In today's world, there are way too many people that try and make every issue about race. It is unfortunate that so many have been deceived and used to sow discord in our communities. We must love one another and move forward in unity, not separation.

Can you imagine if we all truly saw the power we have together rather than apart? Wow! This world would change forever. I may be a bit naive but I don't see the world through any color, race, social status etc… We can be more than what we have become!

Here's another story that you're

> **We can be more than what we have become!**

probably are more familiar with, not as funny but a good one…the woman with the issue of blood. It is told not only twice but three times in 3 different Gospels. It must be pretty important.

True Faith!

Mathew 9:18-22
Mark 5:21-34
Luke 8:40-56

So here it is: While on the way to heal a young girl, Jesus was walking through a crowd pressed on all sides. A woman touched his robe and He immediately knew it was different from all the other people around him. Imagine…knowing one special touch was different from all the rest. I don't think I would know. Would you? He was not angry, He just wanted to teach her about faith.

The woman came to Jesus when He asked, "who touched me?" and she said she touched him because she knew with just a touch she could be healed. What did he say? "Your Faith has healed you!" Nothing like you would expect a human, earthly, pompous king to say, or one full of himself or herself. He did not say, "Are you kidding me, I just had this robe dry cleaned! Why do we have to walk through all of these people anyway? ...Can't they see I'm in a hurry! I don't have time for this! (You know what I'm talking about.) You laugh but we all have experienced some of those thoughts or feelings at some time in our lives.

Faith and love are VERBS

Genuine faith causes action!

There are times of instant healing and times where God allows us to walk through situations to gain healing or deliverance from something else.

Ten years ago my mom was diagnosed with stage 4 aggressive breast cancer. She was healed and has been in remission all these years. She was taught genuine faith; to walk through something where the doctors are saying hope is slim and come out on the other side is a true miracle!

Nevertheless, I will bring health and healing to it; I will heal my people and will let them enjoy abundant peace and security. Jeremiah 33:6

Now faith is confidence in what we hope for and assurance about what we do not see. This is what the ancients were commended for. By faith we understand that the universe was formed at God's command, so that what is seen was not made out of what was visible. Hebrews 11:1-3

Did you know that most of Hebrews chapter 11 begins with the words "By faith"...?

Many times we think of healing as being a health issue but there is more to it. We can find healing in heart issues: abandonment, rejection, depression, or feelings of unworthiness, helplessness and many more.

There is healing from abuse, alcoholism, drug addiction and anything else that can hold us captive from God's best and the abundant life He wants us to live. The great thing is...**you just have to ask and believe**

TRUST

that He can do anything.

Here are some things that we can do to help in the healing process:

1. Admit to yourself and to God there are unresolved hurts in your heart.

2. Give up the right to blame others. Take ownership for any part of an offense done against you.

3. Confess and seek Godly council.

4. Pray a prayer of forgiveness for each person who has hurt you and address each memory or experience. (Truly forgive and let go)

5. Begin steps to heal and restore fellowship with anyone who has offended you.
   - Give up the right to feel angry any longer and give up all negative feelings about them or the situation.
   - Receive that person as they are. (No one is

> People can be unfair & friends may desert us. Trust God!

perfect and we cannot see or know his or her heart.)
- Agree to say only positive and nice things about them (in or out of their presence)
- Respond to them in a loving fashion.
- Pray against the enemy when he tries to attack that situation or relationship. Speak life not death!
- Pray and speak the Word out loud. (It has power to change your perspective and attitude)
- Rest in the Lord and believe in His truths.
- If anything comes back up just pray and say....I have chosen forgiveness and God has taken care of it. I will not pick this back up or go there again! In the name of Jesus.

Sample prayer of forgiveness:
Heavenly Father:

I choose today to forgive _____(fill in the blank). I forgive them for:

_____

_____.

I choose to forgive him / her for the hurt / wrongdoing they have done to me or done in my life. I choose to forgive them unconditionally. I drop every charge against them and I give up my right to ever accuse them of that wrong doing again.

    I no longer will judge them or hold anything over them. I release them from all responsibility for this hurt and I ask forgiveness for taking on this offense. I chose to take this on and it is my responsibility to let it go. I forgive myself for taking on any wrong attitudes, actions, reactions or negative thoughts against _____, and anything associated with this offense. I ask you to forgive me as well.

    Please forgive me God for any thoughts or negative attitudes that I have had against you for allowing this to happen. I know there is evil in this world. You are not the problem but only the solution and hope.

Since I have forgiven_____,
I release him / her from the hurt, bitterness, anger and unforgiveness in my heart. I choose your grace and forgiveness in my life and I choose to walk out my salvation with you daily.

Please heal all of my thoughts, emotions and memories from all the damage this has caused in my life. I choose wholeness and healing. Thank you for my healing Father. I love you, in Jesus' name. Amen.

Let Go and Let God!

Forgiveness is for you NOT them

Chapter Questions

1. How do you feel? Did praying help? Did it reveal more issues or feelings?

2. Are you ready to move forward or are there more issues you feel need to be addressed? If so, STOP and pray.

3. Are there people in your life that have hurt you? Do you still have unforgiveness toward them? Take out a piece of paper and begin writing down names of people that have caused hurt in your life. Now, pray and let God heal those places in your heart.

4. What would your reaction or response be to the person(s) who have hurt you if you ran into them on the street today? If you feel you could greet them with open arms with no thought of the offense then you are moving in the right direction!

When you forgive, you are releasing yourself from bitterness, anger, hurt and pain...

Allowing joy, peace and happiness to come in!

8

The Boldness of Grace

> God is beyond our comprehension & we do not always know why he allows things to happen or come into our lives. Our part is to remain faithful and faith-filled.

Definition of Boldness: *not hesitating or fearful, courageous and daring, beyond the usual limits of conventional thought or action*

The aroma fills the air like a fresh pot of coffee beginning to brew on a sweet winter morning. The sun peeks through the blinds sending a ripple of light across the floor. It awakens our senses and we begin to stir. A smell or a taste brings back memories of childhood or sends us into a tailspin of emotions from past hurts.

There's a place in me that wants to crawl back into bed and retreat. I am not a morning person. My brain does not fully function before 10am so, when my emotions get stirred up early.... well, I definitely want to go back to sleep and start again! How about you?

We just have to remember these are just feelings and emotions. We cannot allow them to rule over us. It is hard not to let emotions take over, especially as a woman. I don't know about you but there have been days when I don't know what page I'm on. I'm sure my husband would say "let me off this emotional train!"

It takes boldness to move ahead, to do something that we are not comfortable with or want to do. God never promised life would be easy! He only promised you would never be alone and He would never forsake you! Isn't that good to know! Sure helps me, especially on those kinds of mornings! Stepping out of our comfort zones requires some boldness on our part.

Just imagine if we locked ourselves up in our room and never came out; just like we can emotionally lock ourselves up to keep others away (or out of our lives). It's easier and we don't get hurt. The flip side is…we never get to experience anything, the gift of friendship, love, adventures and even pain that helps us grow. God's grace is bold and is always covering us allowing growth and so much more - life more abundant than we could ever imagine - even in the embers of loss and disaster.

GRACE on Fire!

When I look back at the last ten months of my life I see how God's grace has given me the boldness to be a voice for my mother. She had to have heart bypass surgery, with complications of a pacemaker and a stroke, she was not able to speak or take care of herself. I began the journey of her primary caregiver, 24/7 for a few weeks then daily 6 days a week and finally tapering down to a few days a week etc.... She is working to make it back as a strong independent woman. Can you imagine what it would be like? You have no control over anything and you couldn't take care of yourself? Most of us shutter at the thought of having no control. We hang up "pretty"

Give in and let it go.

towels in the guest bathroom and our husband tries to wipe his dirty hands on it. You yell "stop, don't use those…they're for guest!" He so doesn't get it!

Give in and let go! I'm not sure I like that saying much. My flesh says no but my spirit and heart say yes. I get it! When God calls us to let go of things that are out of our control we must comply. It can "derail us from our destiny!"

When things are out of control I find myself in a whirlwind spiraling down. God's grace gives me the strength and peace to let go and to move forward into His plans for me; although, they are not always what I had planned.

"I'm undone in your presence Lord, your grace surrounds me and covers me; a shelter from the rain / "reign" around me. Swirling tumultuous waves of pain, weariness try to engulf me with emotions. This is the place in which I have been for ten months.

My grace is sufficient for you, for my

power is made perfect in weakness. Therefore I will boast all the more gladly about my weaknesses, so that Christ's power may rest on me. That is why, for Christ's sake, I delight in my weaknesses; in insults, in hardships, in persecution, in difficulties. For when I am weak He is strong." II Corinthians 12:9-10

> True friends accept you in the good and bad times.

As a young Christian in my teens I learned that talking about my weaknesses, my problems etc.... was complaining and wrong. I was to suffer in silence, bear my own pain and be happy. I strived for perfection and never spoke to anyone about anything. As an adult I have learned that true relationships can handle "truth". Times of hardship and pain should be shared and walked out with others of like-mindedness. It's ok to admit and talk about what you are going through. Those who understand and are willing to listen, talk and pray with you are those who "get it". We should seek wise counsel and walk out life together. That's how God designed it.

"See to it that no one takes you captive through hollow and deceptive philosophy, which depends on human tradition and the basic principles of this world rather than on Christ." Colossians 2:8

Paul says..."I want you to know how much I am struggling for you and for those at Laodicea, and for all those who have not met me personally. My purpose is that they may be encouraged in heart and united love, so that they may have the riches of Christ in whom all are hidden the treasures of wisdom and knowledge." Colossians 2:1-3

Isn't it amazing, Paul can admit his struggles but yet we can't? When we struggle, it isn't a sign of weakness but strength. We must have a pliable heart and willing spirit to change.
Something has gone wrong in our society and churches. So many times the church has labeled someone or even run him / her out of the church because "they asked for prayer too much or were too needy." Wow...I

> People's acceptance or rejection or us is not the measure of our success.

love that one. Is not the church a place where people come to find healing, deliverance, fellowship, understanding etc.? It's made up of "people". Imperfect people, people with flaws, people in need of a Savior! Yes, even in leadership! We are not judge and jury. We do not "throw the baby out with the bath water!" It comes back to control; with some - even entitlement and power.

I want to impress upon you how important it is to Love! How many times did Jesus say to "love" or "Love one another"? 11 Times to Love One Another. Love: 311 in the Old Testament and 180 in the New Testament, 51 times when He was walking this earth and 2 times in Revelation. That seems important to me! When we let go of control and begin focusing on others outside of ourselves we begin to have "eyes like Jesus". I want to have my Father's eyes to see people they way He does – with Love and compassion extending GRACE. Loving beyond measure!

"Instead, speaking the truth in love,

we will in all things grow up into him who is the Head, that is, Christ. From him the whole body, joined and held together by every supporting ligament, grows and builds itself up in love, as each part does its work. I tell you this, and insist on it in the Lord, that you must no longer live as the Gentiles do, in the futility of their thinking. They are darkened in their understanding and separated from the life of God because of the ignorance that is in them due to the hardening of their hearts...." Ephesians 4:15-19

"Brothers do not slander one another. Anyone who speaks against his brother or judges him speaks against the law and judges it. When you judge the law, you are not keeping it, but sitting in judgment on it. There is only one Lawgiver and Judge, the one who is able to save and destroy. But you, who are you to judge." James 4:11-12

This is Grace on Fire!

Let go of control!

This is all apart of boldness. **Living life out loud! Not fearful but hopeful! With Faith not faithless!** When we walk in the fullness of grace, we let go of our control and let God! Let God…what does that look like in your life? Be still a moment in the silence and ask God what it really looks like?

Don't walk away or give up. God wants to do something extraordinary in your life. *Do not do the "usual" and skim over these important life lessons and teachings to move on to something else.* If we truly can grasp the truth of loving and letting go we can begin to walk in the fullness of life that God truly desires for us! He is waiting. Will you let Him in? Will you let Him do heart surgery and weed out the unwanted weeds from years of hurt, pain, anger or disappointment? He wants complete healing for you and loves you so much that He has given His grace to cover a multitude of sin to see you healthy, happy and whole.

"Let us then approach the throne of grace with confidence, so that we may receive mercy and find grace to help us in our time of need."
Hebrews 4:16

I know that it will be difficult letting go but you can do it! I have been there and I am still walking it out right along with you. Hang in there and know that the God of all creation has created you to love and be whole. You are loved! Believe it and receive it!

Let's Pray:
Lord God, I am undone in your presence. I love how you love me and even if I fully don't understand all that you have for me, I give up control of_____
and I release it to you. I know that there will be times where I want to pick this up again but please help me to apply your grace and remember that you have called be to be healed and whole. I surrender to your will and give up mine. Help me see others the way you see them and not judge

or "look over" those in need. I want to love unconditionally and treat others the way I want to be treated. Help me to walk in boldness and not fear, speaking truth but always in love. Draw me close to you as I search for your truth in my life. You are my rock and my salvation and you deliver me in times of need when I put my trust and faith in you. I choose to set my eyes on you. I choose to set my heart toward you. Your love is great and I am thankful for all you are doing in my life. In Jesus' name. Amen.

Chapter Questions — Move out of your comfort zone!

1. Where are your comfort zones? How can you make changes in those areas?

2. In what areas are you content with being in control? What steps are you going to take to let go? Can you let go and let God take over and wash over you with His grace? Why or why not?

3. Can you remember a time when the storms of life were swirling around you? (Maybe you are there now.) Do you see God moving in those times? Have you given God permission to move? Why or why not?

4. Have you experienced hurt in the local church? What happened? Look deep into your heart and be honest.... was this hurt from people in the church or your expectations of people in the church? You should have true relationships within your church, not the Sunday hello and Wednesday "how are you" and leave. Ask the Lord to bring true relationships and fellowship into your life where it is needed.

5. Do you roar like a lion or whimper like a mouse? Do you walk in boldness or bluntness? Walking in boldness does not mean saying everything that you think. Are you using your boldness to stand up for what you believe in? Are you a voice for those who do not have one? Ask God for direction to be bold and to walk it out in love. How does that look in your life?

Live by God's standards even when society says otherwise

9

The Circle of Grace

'Round and 'round it goes…over and over the scenery never changes. It spins and moves in time to the music that swirls about, lights flicker, everything passes by in a blur. That's what life can be. It's as if we are on a merry – go - round. We are still but everything else is moving at a very fast pace. Faces and places are unrecognizable.

I am thankful that grace is not like that at all. *"Steady grace that keeps forgiving; giving us a steady heart that keeps on growing and going. We begin to have a steady faith that keeps on believing. (Grace through our circumstances, grace through our weaknesses, grace through the rain, grace through the pain etc.…)"* God always meets us were we are!

I think of a circle and it is a never-ending line that continues endlessly. On paper, an eraser can only break a circle drawn in pencil. God is that eraser. Have you ever made a presumptuous promise? Sure, I think we all have at some time in our life, not even thinking about what we are saying. When we have been hurt we tend to look for ways to protect ourselves from being hurt again. We might say, "I will never allow this to happen again." We initiate this on our own out of fear or anger. These promises are not made to God but to ourselves. These kinds of statements can be a command that begins to control us, whether we are aware of it or not.

Here are some good examples (maybe you have said some of these as well): "I'll never marry a man like my father!" "I'll never discipline my kids the way my parents did."

"I'll never let them get the best of me again."

"I'll never………." (you fill in the

> Don't harden your heart from people

blank)

God is calling me by name

"Casting down imaginations and every high thing that exalts itself against the knowledge of God, and bringing it into captivity every thought to the obedience of Christ."
II Corinthians 10:5

Our lives should be guided by the Holy Spirit, not by rash decisions or outbursts. Remember whatever we put in our minds and hearts will come out and it begins to play like videotape in our lives. (Over and over)

Also, there are generational issues / curses (things passed on from parents, grandparents etc.....) that continue to infiltrate our lives over and over. There are many reasons why generational issues are still visible and alive and well in our lives. First, there could be un-repentance, a breaking of covenant with God or walking in the footsteps of your father or mother. If we choose to see what is happening and repent, we will be healed and delivered! Secondly, there could be sin or a willful ignorance

Let God do heart surgery!

about what is happening. Third, maybe there was a violation that happened. There was an abuse or domination over us. Maybe, no justice was given, questions of doubt…"where was God when this happened?" Any violation done to you by someone else can deeply affect you.

"…so that the body of Christ may be built up until we all reach unity in the faith and in the knowledge of the Son of God and become mature, attaining to the whole measure of the fullness of Christ. Then we will no longer be infants, tossed back and forth by the waves and blown here and there by every wild teaching and by the cunning and craftiness of men in their deceitful scheming." Ephesians 4:13-14

"Therefore, my dear friends, as you have always obeyed-not only in my presence, but now much more in my absence-continue to work out your salvation (this was written for the church to work together to rid themselves of division and discord)

with fear and trembling, for it is God who works in you to will and act accordingly to his good purpose. Do everything without complaining or arguing, so that you may become blameless and pure, children of God without fault in a crooked and depraved generation, in which you shine like stars in the universe as you hold out the word of life in order that I may boast on the day of Christ that I did not run or labor for nothing. But even if I am being poured out like a drink offering on the sacrifice and service coming from your faith, I am glad and rejoice with all of you. So you too should be glad and rejoice with me." Philippians 2:12-18

As I think about God's unending love and forever promises I am reminded of Abraham and Sarah. (Genesis 21:1-7) Who would have believed that Abraham would have a son at 100 years of age and live to raise him to adulthood? Also, Sarah his wife was barren and could not have children. But, God does the impossible everyday. Our problems will not seem as big if we let God handle them. Let's think about what Sarah went through. After repeated promises and a visit by angels and the appearance from the Lord himself, Sarah finally cried out with surprise and joy at the birth of her son Isaac. But, because of her doubt, worry and fear, she had forfeited the peace she could have felt in the promise given to her.

Have you ever worried yourself sick over something or someone? I try not to be a worrier but sometimes it gets the best of me. I worry that my children are not making good choices, especially when I am not around. I find myself worrying over little things like, "are my children taking care of their teeth, going to the doctor, eating right etc.... Then of course, the big ones... are they keeping their relationship with Jesus, finding a church home, not having premarital sex, doing drugs and drinking etc.... I have found that I am not the only one feeling this way. I did for a long time because it wasn't the "thing" to do.... actually vocalizing my worries or trials of life."

God's got this...

Don't worry

No one wanted to hear it and seemed as though it was wrong and I was less than or lacking in some way. Have you been there? I feel like I'm losing my mind sometimes but then God reminds me of who He is and that He came to give peace not fear! The way to bring peace to our troubled heart is to focus on God's promises. Trust is the key. We must trust him to see the fullness of peace in our lives. Do not allow your peace and joy to be taken.

"We demolish arguments and every pretension that sets itself up against the knowledge of God, and we take captive every thought to make it obedient to Christ."
2 Corinthians 10:5

Some of the lessons that Sarah learned in her life were that God responds to faith even in the midst of failure. Also, God is not bound by what usually happens, he can stretch the limits, break through walls we have put up over the years and cause unheard of events to happen! He is able to do great and mighty thing in our lives if we let him.

"By faith Abraham, even though he was past age-and Sarah herself was barren-was enable to become a father because he considered him faithful who had made the promise. And so from this man, and he as good as dead, came descendants as numerous as the stars in the sky and as countless as the sand on the seashore." Hebrews 11:11-12

"Now the Lord was gracious to Sarah as he had said, and the Lord did for Sarah what he had promised." Genesis 21:1

Sarah had trouble believing Gods promises for her. She also attempted to work out her problems for herself without consulting God and she also tried to cover her faults by blaming others. Have you ever done any of those things? (I know I have) It's in our weakness God shows himself strong! Even with all of her weaknesses, God gave Sarah a child

> What does it really mean to take a leap of faith?

through her barrenness. The circle of faithlessness and doubt was broken.

Grace on fire!

We do not have to live in the same circle or cycles that we are accustom to. We can break the cycle by faith, praying and letting God take over. Remember when we let go and let God - it doesn't mean the subject or issue will never come up again. It means when it does, we can give it to God and say "I have given this to you and I refuse to step back into old patterns, crisis's etc...." whatever has held you back or has a hold on you. By staying in God's word, praying and having a relationship with him it will help you stay on track and focused.

"...Let us throw off everything that hinders and the sin that so easily entangles and let us run with perseverance the race marked our for us. Let us fix our eyes on Jesus, the author and perfecter of our faith, who for the joy set before him endured the cross, scorning its shame and sat down at the right

hand of the throne of God. Consider him who endured such opposition from sinful men, so that you will not grow weary and lose heart." Hebrews 12:1-3

My old patterns are turning to food in times of stress or walking away and giving up. Life can be hard. It's not easy to walk the narrow road and stay focused straight ahead. It's much easier to grab fast food and lie around after a long stressful and stress filled day. I don't know about you but I like food and by the end of the day I am wiped! I have tried the 5am running and all the fad diets known to man. I don't like fried foods and dairy is not my friend. You would think I would be skinny with just that! I'm just keeping it real. It's a daily struggle and I have not won this battle yet but I have faith that when I truly let go and let God have the wheel, I will overcome and beat this!

His Grace is sufficient even in my struggles so I know it is in yours! My prayer is that we all realize and truly understand the reality of God's grace

I am an OVERCOMER!

Be encouraged and stay strong!

and how we can walk confident in His truths and in freedom when we truly let go and embrace them! He has promised that we overcome by the blood of the lamb and the word of our testimony. Let's be transparent and share what we are going through so we can find healing and wholeness through God's great grace! We can do this together.

Let's allow God's grace to catch fire in our hearts!

Chapter Questions

1. Have you ever made any promises or vows like the ones early in the chapter? "I'll never_____, etc...." Look back at some of the examples if you need some help.

2. Promises or vows such as these can hinder us. EX: "I'll never let anyone hurt me like that again." This hardens your heart, makes you shut down and never open up to love or friendships again. Write down some things you have said and how they have affected your life.

3. In what ways have you tried to undo these vows? Have you let go of any? If so, how has it brought freedom into your life? **Let down the walls!**

4. Let's think about generational issues. Think back and try to remember events or people that have wronged or hurt you. Also, anyone in your family that has abused you, has drug or alcohol issues etc.... These kinds of things can hold you back, make you put up walls, cause you not to trust or make you push people away etc.... Write these events/issues down.

5. Now, let's pray and let those events, people or generational issues go!

Forgiveness (just in case you want to go through it again, as in Chapter 7)

Heavenly Father:
I choose today to forgive_____
(fill in the blank).
I forgive them for: _____
_____.
I choose to forgive him/her for the hurt /wrong doing that they have done to me or done in my life. I choose to forgive them unconditionally. I drop every charge against them and I give up my right to ever accuse them of that wrongdoing again.

I no longer will judge them or hold anything over them. I release them from all responsibility for this hurt and I ask forgiveness for taking on this offense. I chose to take this on and it is my responsibility to let it go. I forgive myself for taking on any wrong attitudes, actions, reactions or negative thoughts against _____, and anything associated with this offense. I ask you to forgive me as well. Please forgive me God for any thoughts or negative attitudes that I have had against you for allowing this to happen. I know that bad things happen and you do not cause them and that there is evil in this world. You are not the problem but only the solution and hope.

Since I have forgiven_____,
I release him/her from the hurt, bitterness, anger and unforgiveness in my heart. I choose your grace and forgiveness in my life and I choose to walk out my salvation with you daily.

Please heal all of my thoughts, emotions and memories from all the damage that this has caused in my life. I choose wholeness and healing. Thank you for my healing Father. I love you, in Jesus' name. Amen.

Vows/Issues

Father, I also break the generational curse / issue of_____ in Jesus Name! Also, the vow that I made_____. I release all ties and bonds with it and I ask that you cover my family and generations to come with a hedge of protection against these former issues. When I see these issues come up, I will choose to run the other direction. I will not pick it up and carry it like a badge of honor nor will I give it the attention it desires. I will claim victory and walk in the knowledge that you are a keeper of your word. You say that it will not return void. I give it to you and that's it…. it's done. Thank you for your saving and unfaltering grace. I love you. In Jesus' name. Amen!

6. Are you a worrier? What things do you worry about on a daily, weekly or regular basis? What adjustments can you make to not stay in this same pattern?

10

The Edge of Grace

I looked up the word edge and there are so many but I like this one…"on the brink or verge."

The edge of my reality looks dim. The vast caverns below beckon with the wind. I feel as though time has stopped and waited for me with abated breath. The pounding of my heart awakens the silence around me. I tremble in fear with the thought of it coming to an end but the end is nowhere in sight. If I take one more step…snap I break, it all comes crashing down.

That's reality at times. As I write this book my reality is stress filled days of managing two households, taking care of a sick parent and all of her needs, my middle son just moved to Indiana, we put in hardwood floors, I was injured during a trip, running my own business, part time ministry, teaching my daughter to drive and helping her get her license and preparing for college applications! Oh and my oldest son is serving our country for the next nine months overseas. Do you think that is enough plates spinning for now? It's all the things that have to get done or to be concerned about. I think we all have months even years like this at times. Right now, I always say…

"Can we stop this train, I want to get off?"

> Just keep holding on.

There never seems to be enough time in the day, there is an endless attack from every side. One day, it hit! In the middle of a T-Mobile store, I received a call and on the other end was a home health care facility that is supposed to be helping with my mom and she begins to yell at me and blame everyone else for all that is going wrong. I lost it. Have you ever lost it…really lost it?

I hung up on her because I was so angry. I began to sob hysterically in the middle of the store. Everyone was watching me as I tried to speak through the tears... "I'll just come back later.... sob, sob, sob... just forget it, sob, sob, sob ...just give me back the phone, sob, sob, sob ..." I got into the car and of course had to call my husband.... sob, sob, sob. This was my edge. My reality was coming to a crashing halt and I wanted to jump! Am I the only one?

I wanted someone to fix it and I wanted life back to normal well, "my normal". I wanted life to be easy and fun. I wanted everything to go right and not have to take care of everything. I was done. To top it all off, I felt alone as if I were doing all of this by myself. My husband helped when he could but there were no friends or family reaching out to help. That was the icing on the cake.

I have felt abandoned by friends of 20+ years when I was always there to sit at their bedside during cancer surgeries, doctor visits, accidents, held their hair as they got sick, baby-sitting kids, bringing meals etc..... even when I did not have time. I thought "Wow, when I need them....

> **People will fail you but God never will leave you or forsake you**

they were not there." Yes, I reached out, sent text, emails and calls to let them know. Crazy, huh? Yes, it's not right and it's not fair. (We also have to realize that some people are just not able to meet felt needs because they do not have to ability or capacity to help. Sometimes they are so focused on their own life that the never see outside of their own world and sometimes their love tank is just as empty as yours.)

Life is not always going to turn out the way that you want or think it should. Once again, it was God and me to weather the storms of life. But God reminded me as I was standing on my cliff, dangling my feet off the edge: **Instead of standing on the edge of a cliff about to fall or break it's actually the "brink or verge", the edge, of a breakthrough!**

"God is about to give you something better or bigger; more than you could ever imagine! He is making you stronger and able to carry all that He has for you! So, even in the darkness there is light. He has a plan to make everything work for His glory

and your good!"

Really God? That's hard to believe. I struggled with...why? Focusing on other people and how I needed someone to come alongside and help me. He said...I'm here! But, I need...."I'm here! But, you don't understand...."Sherri, I'm here!" But....

"No, I'm here!"

Do you get what God is saying? Sometimes we don't truly hear God because we are too busy crying...poor me or why me etc....? I had to stop focusing on what I didn't have and more on what I did have! If you are walking through something like that, stop and be mindful of the positives and what God has given you in your life. Whatever you are going through, He is able and His grace will cover you through it all!

Grace on fire and on the brink of breakthrough!

So do not throw away your confidence; it will be richly

Keep pressing forward!

rewarded. You need to persevere so that when you have done the will of God, you will receive what he has promised. For, "In just a little while, he who is coming will come and will not delay. And, "But my righteous one will live by faith. And I take no pleasure in the one who shrinks back." But we do not belong to those who shrink back and are destroyed, but to those who have faith and are saved. Hebrews 10:35-39

Let us not become weary in doing good, for at the proper time we will reap a harvest if we do not give up. Galatians 6:9

But as for you, be strong and do not give up, for your work will be rewarded." 2 Chronicles 15:7

The wonderful thing about grace is it has no end. There is no stopping grace when God has given it. As His child I am covered by it. It doesn't mean that I walk around doing whatever I want, whenever I want. If we don't stay under the covering of God we will get

> Grace has no end.

wet. (like an umbrella on a rainy day…we stay under it, we stay dry and protected.) I love how God's grace forgives and wipes the slate clean as we ask for forgiveness. It sees imperfections and doesn't judge, only extends its hand in love.

I think about the edge of something and I think about boundaries. I come to an impassable edge and stop. There's no way to get across or pass so, what do I do…I turn around and go back the same way I came.

What? But, our destination is on the other side. There is only one way and that is across a deep cavern. Looking from the edge it is impossible. We can't cross, there's no bridge. A small voice is calling in the distance…Take a step; you just can't see it yet. "What?" "Are you crazy?" "I'm not stepping out into nothingness." The voice says, "Trust me, it is there." "I have given you a bridge. You just don't see it because you are lacking in faith." You recognize the voice and you begin to step. Your ground is solid as you make your way across. Your

Let God take you to the other side.

confidence is building and you begin to run! When you arrive, you look back only to see the bridge. You no longer see the edge of the cliff, it is but a distant memory.

God has given us all bridges and a way to make it to the other side. He is that way. Your faith and trust in him will make a way when there seems to be no way. He is the way maker!

For years I have heard a saying...."Build a bridge and get over it." I think it rightly applies. We have to allow God to build it so we can have breakthrough. You can do it! Whatever you are going through, He will make a way. Keep moving forward and place on foot in front of the other.

God never promised life to be easy just that we would never walk it alone. (Even if we feel alone...He is always there)

Faith in Action!

Stay the course!

Chapter Questions

1. Are you on your edge? Have you ever gone through so many things at once that you lost it? Name some of those times and how you dealt with it.

2. Let's write down some ways to get off our edge and step out in faith.

3. Have you ever felt abandoned by friends, family etc....? Are you in a place of forgiveness and letting go or holding onto the past? If you are still holding on, stop and pray. Let God take that disappointment, hurt, rejection etc.... and let Him build your bridge to wholeness and healing. Write down what God is saying to you right now. (Who do you need to forgive?)

God wants to heal your broken heart

11

Eyes of Grace

"The eye is the lamp of the body. If your eyes are healthy, your whole body will be full of light.
Matthew 6:22

God's loving eyes are always watching. He sees my best and my worst. I know there is nothing I can do to take away His love for me. His graceful and merciful eyes are watching in times of sorrow as well.

As a teen I lost my grandmother and grandfather within the same year and I have lost friends to cancer and other family members along the way. Nothing could prepare me for the loss of my little brother at the age of 18.

I was 23 and living in Houston when I heard a loud crash in the middle of the night. It woke me up from a dead sleep but no one else heard the loud noise. I thought it might be the sound of a train crash. The sound was so loud and clear. My heart was racing. Shortly after I awoke, at 2am, the phone rang. I began to cry and told my "soon to be" husband that something happened to my mom or someone in Dallas. Jeff's mom answered the phone and gave it to me. It was as if time had stopped and everything was going in slow motion. My mom was crying hysterically but through the tears her words pierced my heart. My brother had been in a car accident with some friends.

The crash I heard in my spirit was at the exact time of the car accident in which my brother had been killed. I knew something had happened. I was in shock as I packed my bags and got dressed. I had to go to Dallas to be with my mom. Jeff drove the 4 long hours as I sat in the passenger seat crying. Was this real? Could this really be happening? You hear about these kind of things but you really never think about them happening to you or your family. Over the next few

His peace comes in the morning - mourning

days and weeks I had a recurring song that God sung to me. He said my eye is on the sparrow so if I am watching him, I am certainly watching you. I am here, Sherri.

Why should I be discouraged and why should the shadows come?
Why should my heart be lonely and long for heaven and home?
When Jesus is my portion, a constant Friend is He,
His eye is on the sparrow and I know He watches me.
His eye is on the sparrow and I know He watches me.

I sing because I'm happy;
I sing because I'm free;
His eye is on the sparrow
And I know He watches me.

Let not your heart be troubled; these tender words I hear; and resting on his goodness I lose my doubts and fears;
For by the path He leadeth but one step I may see; His eye is on the sparrow and I know He watches me.

He is my portion. He's all I'll ever need.

*His eye is on the sparrow and I know
He watches me.*

Whenever I am tempted; whenever clouds arise; when songs give place to sighing; when hope within me dies; I draw thee closer to Him; from care He sets me free; His eye is on the sparrow and I know He watches me. His eye is on the sparrow and I know He watches me.

*I sing because I'm happy;
I sing because I'm free;
His eye is on the sparrow
And I know He watches me...*

These words were a comfort along with knowing that God is in control no matter the situation. We do not always understand or know why God allows things to happen but my faith is not shaken by happenings in this world. I have the hope in Christ Jesus that gives me strength. God's grace is always there, surrounding us especially in our time of sorrow.

I would need God's grace once again when my mom was diagnosed

> It seems to all hit at once but with God we can handle anything.

with stage four-breast cancer with 26 lymph nodes involved. She drove herself to Chemo then to work three or four times a week. To this day, I don't know how she did it. It was God's grace! During Chemo, mom moved in with us, fell and broke her leg and I began driving her to treatments and to daily radiation. She went through a hard time. She could not do anything for herself. 6-8 weeks of radiation and she was done. It has been 8+ years and she is still cancer free!

Grace on Fire!

His eyes are always watching and keeping care. She recently had heart surgery where there were complications. Her heart stopped, a pacemaker was put in to help her heart function, two stints, a major valve replacement and she had a stroke. The long 6 weeks in the hospital, skilled nursing and now home health care is taking its toll on all of us. Even through all of this we know that God has never left us or forsaken us. He is the reason we have hope and that she is still here with us.

Even though I walk through the darkest valley, I will fear no evil, for you are with me; your rod and your staff, they comfort me. Psalm 23:4

Shout for joy, you heavens; rejoice, you earth; burst into song, you mountains! For the Lord comforts his people and will have compassion on his afflicted ones.
Isaiah 49:13

As you know, we count as blessed those who have persevered. You have heard of Job's perseverance and have seen what the Lord finally brought about. The Lord is full of compassion and mercy. James 5:11

When I think about how compassionate God has been, I can't help but think about the state of this world and how so many have no grace in their eyes. God sees all of us the same. There are no differences in culture, color, class etc.… **We are all His creation**. So many have turned

> **Live in unity together and be compassionate**

their heart against people living a sinful lifestyle, they have spewed hatred because of different beliefs or even skin color. If we are to make a difference in this world we must have love and compassion for one another!

Finally, all of you, be like-minded, be sympathetic, love one another, be compassionate and humble.
1 Peter 3:8

I have no understanding for the political lies and gains, those who treat injustice as an excuse to break the law, vandalize and spew hatred. I have no understanding for those who think they are above the law and those who harass or belittle others.

Furthermore, why lie? Can we be a people of our word? Can we see others the way that God sees them? Can there be no racial disputes? Can we truly love beyond our faults and without measure? **These are hard questions that our world needs to get.** It starts with us; each individual accepting responsibility for his or her own actions, thoughts and lifestyle.

Live in peace with love.

Now, I am not saying that we should be ok with sin but we can love people and stand in truth without shoving judgment down their throat at every turn. I am sure they will not see who God truly is through the judgmental plank in our eye. We have all sinned and none of us are perfect.

Although, we do have a choice; God is a gentleman and He will not force himself on us. We must choose! We have a freewill and when things don't go our way it does not give us a license for lawlessness. We shouldn't go around destroying property or looting. What good is violence? Has violence or hatred ever been effective? NO.

It is ludicrous to think that violence; hatred, judgment etc....would have any other outcome than the same.

The only way to find peace is to find it in your self through Christ. Can you imagine if everyone took responsibility over himself or herself and began seeing each other as God sees…Grace, what wonderful grace would abound.

TRUTH

How can you say to your brother, 'Brother, let me take the speck out of your eye,' when you yourself fail to see the plank in your own eye? You hypocrite, first take the plank out of your eye, and then you will see clearly to remove the speck from your brother's eye. Luke 6:42

Repent, then, and turn to God, so that your sins may be wiped out, that times of refreshing may come from the Lord. Acts 3:19

For all have sinned and fall short of the glory of God. Romans 3:23

What shall we say, then? Shall we go on sinning so that grace may increase? Romans 6:1

By no means! We are those who have died to sin; how can we live in it any longer? Romans 6:2

For we know that our old self was

crucified with him so that the body ruled by sin might be done away with, that we should no longer be slaves to sin. Romans 6:6

Because anyone who has died has been set free from sin. Romans 6:7

For we know that since Christ was raised from the dead, he cannot die again; death no longer has mastery over him. Romans 6:9

The death he died, he died to sin once for all; but the life he lives, he lives to God. Romans 6:10

In the same way, count yourselves dead to sin but alive to God in Christ Jesus. Romans 6:11

Therefore do not let sin reign in your mortal body so that you obey its evil desires. Romans 6:12

Do not offer any part of yourself to sin as an instrument of wickedness, but rather offer yourselves to God as those who have been brought from death to life; and offer every part of yourself to him as an instrument of righteousness. Romans 6:13

For sin shall no longer be your master, because you are not under the law, but under grace.
Romans 6:14

What then? Shall we sin because we are not under the law but under grace? By no means! Romans 6:15

Don't you know that when you offer yourselves to someone as obedient slaves, you are slaves of the one you obey—whether you are slaves to sin, which leads to death, or to obedience, which leads to righteousness? Romans 6:16

But thanks be to God that, though you used to be slaves to sin, you have come to obey from your heart the pattern of teaching that has now claimed your allegiance.
Romans 6:17

You have been set free from sin and

have become slaves. When you were slaves to sin, you were free from the control of righteousness.
Romans 6:18

But now that you have been set free from sin and have become slaves of God, the benefit you reap leads to holiness, and the result is eternal life. Romans 6:22

GRACE

For the wages of sin is death, but the gift of God is eternal life in Christ Jesus our Lord. Romans 6:23

Remember, when we are judgmental, hateful etc.... we are sinning as well. All of these things are a big deal to God. Sin is sin and truth is truth, no matter how hard to swallow. The good news is "we can be forgiven" and turn our lives around and change our world.

    I want to be a world changer! How about you? I have sinned many times and I do not claim to be perfect but by the grace of God, I am forgiven when I come to him and repent. I love how God is so gracious that He allows "do overs"! How about you?

Let us have eyes of grace to see as God sees. I want my Father's eyes to see beyond the natural and into the heart.

I want grace to catch like fire.

Chapter Questions

1. When have you felt your best? When have you been at your worst?

2. Write down any events that have had you in a tailspin or times when you have felt helpless.

3. How did you respond during those times? Did you shut down or run away? Did you rest your faith in Jesus? What would you do differently now if anything? What did you learn during those times?

4. Have you ever passed judgment or been hateful to someone? If so, explain... Why did you act this way? What do you think has caused you to respond the same way over and over?

5. Do you still have a judgmental attitude or hateful spirit toward anyone or group etc....? Who or what? Why?

6. How can you be healed or overcome these feelings or thoughts? Stop and pray and let God heal those places. As God leads, you may want to ask a specific person for forgiveness as well. (It takes much maturity and humility to do this. I have been there and it was very healing for me.)

12

Days of Grace

It's darkest just before the dawn. The lack of light causes me to trip and fall. I stumble on feeble legs and I'm blinded by the black of night. I never see it coming, a hit out of nowhere. Hard left then right, I turn and I'm hit again. Over and over until relief.... light breaks through. Its momentary brightness helps me to stand and shake it off. Wham! The night beckons and it begins again. Will it stop? Why does this continue to happen? Crying out in the night the light finally overtakes its predator. Breathe...dawn has broken.

The surge of lies and attacks in life can be brutal. I know, I've been there. I worked 5 years as an executive assistant and experienced this first hand. One of the executives had issues with me early on. My experience with some of my co-workers was horrible. Several years of lies and gossip about things I did or said that were totally untrue. I was written up for things when I did nothing wrong etc....

After the last attack and lie was spread, I finally gave my notice. Even on the day I turned in my notice, I was once again, reprimanded for something I did not do or say.

It broke my heart when my direct boss never stood up for me or even asked if any of these things were true. "They must be true because they came from an executive staff member, right?" Crazy, huh? The hits and jabs kept coming. The one thing I counted on was God! He knew the truth and my heart. It did not matter about their lies, accusations, assumptions or thoughts about me. But, when the lies of the enemy begin to break you...enough is enough! The grace had lifted to take it any longer. I always say "when the grace lifts, it might be time to move."

I allowed my spirit to be broken. I

Is it easier to believe lies than truth?

did not understand why this was happening and I never spoke up for myself. I figured they had made up their mind and there was nothing I could do to change it so, I kept quiet and pressed on.

For the eyes of the Lord are on the righteous and his ears are attentive to their prayer, but the face of the Lord is against those who do evil. 1 Peter 3:12

He loves us through the darkness to the other side

I share this with you only to show God's grace and goodness. Even through this storm God was showing up and blessing me in other ways. I was given a grand piano and many other things along with blessing my part time ministry outside of my 9 to 5 job. There was definite evidence of God moving when I felt like I was dying inside.

Hurricanes and tornadoes cut and tear everything apart but only strong foundations survive their fury. Those same foundations can be used to rebuild after the storm. A strong foundation is critical. Can you imagine what Job went through? He lost everything. A rags – to - riches - to - rags - to - riches story. He was assaulted on every side, devastated and stripped down to his foundation.

Job was living in the land of Uz and had thousands of sheep, cattle, a large family and many servants. Job lost is children, his possessions and was covered in sores. His wife tried to convince him to curse God but he stayed the course and continued to have faith. His friends told him it was because of his sin he lost everything and was ill. They told him to confess his sin and turn back to God.

It wasn't the truth and his friends finally fell silent. God spoke through a storm and Job fell down in humble reverence for God. In the end Job's wealth and happiness was returned and God rebuked the people who spoke against him.

Does God pervert justice? Does the Almighty pervert what is right? When your children sinned against him, he gave them over to the penalty of their sin. But if you will seek God earnestly and plead with the

Almighty, if you are pure and upright, even now he will rouse himself on your behalf and restore you to your prosperous state. Your beginnings will seem humble, so prosperous will your future be.
Job 8:1-8

"Brothers, in the patience of suffering, take the prophets who spoke in the name of the Lord. As you know, we consider blessed those who have persevered. You have heard of Job's perseverance and have seen what the Lord finally brought about. The Lord is full of compassion and mercy."
James 5:10-11

It's easy to think that we have all the answers but in reality only God knows why things happen as they do. Can you imagine how Job felt? Wow, what faith. I might have quivered back and forth a bit through it all.
Sometimes people are harsh, unfair, liars, unjust, gossips, hypocrites etc.... We all have faced some of these. Standing on a firm foundation will get you through. Handling trials

through grace will be hard but it will be worth it. God's grace is sufficient and He will sustain you when you need it most!

His Grace is on fire!

We all need grace throughout our day. Someone cuts you off on the freeway, or cuts in front of you in line. How about the screaming child in the grocery store? Keeping your head or cool is grace. Extending grace in every situation or to people is not always easy. Especially, when you know you are right! Just saying…

The thing is, we can't be "right fighters", you know - no matter what…"I'm right" and you must acknowledge it. We have all met one before. If we walked around like that all the time we would make ourselves sick.

Suffering can be a part of life, but is not always a penalty of sin. In the same way prosperity is not always a reward for being good. Those who put their trust in God are never promised a life without trouble. We may not fully understand the pain we

> **It is not always because of my sins that trials come**

> **No matter how bleak our situation or how evil the world seems, we must continue to be God's faithful people who hope for His restoration**

experience but it can lead us to rediscover God.

We cannot control the attacks on our lives but we can choose how we respond!
We have to have grace in and out of trials.

No matter what your situation, and we all have them…. don't give up, keep coming back and keep getting up no matter how many times you are knocked down. We cannot let pride get in our way.

We always have difficult situations in life but I had never truly experienced anything more difficult than disagreements, stress, normal life stuff etc.… until I went through a fire. When my oldest, was born we lived in a 2-bedroom apartment on the first floor. One night while I was up nursing I heard this loud screaming. I looked outside to find a naked man on the balcony across the street and I saw smoke coming out of his door. He was screaming, "Call the fire department, help!" I proceeded to wake up Jeff, throw the baby bag together, grab my bible and wedding ring (maybe a few pictures) and out the door we went with the baby to grandmas.

Later we laughed about it for years..."why didn't he put some clothes on, a robe.... something!" We never understood why someone would go to his or her balcony naked and screaming. It just made us laugh every time we thought about it.

Well, turn about is fair play...2009 (Ryan was a Junior) he and my daughter Peyton were staying with friends. Our middle son, Cole was the only one home. It was New Years morning. I had just woken up, taken my pjs off and put on a robe to take a shower.

I stopped and decided to make Jeff breakfast instead. So, I headed to the kitchen (In a three bedroom apartment) to make hash browns. I placed oil in the (metal) pan and turned on the electric stove. I have never cooked on an electric stove therefore, I did not know it heats up much faster and will burn quicker.

Oh how time flies.

> We may be knocked down but we are not taken out!

Suddenly, nature called. I ran to the bathroom just for a moment and the fire alarm went off. My husband had just awakened (pjs off, of course) threw on his robe and ran to the kitchen, which was now engulfed in flames to the ceiling. He freaked out, pulled off his robe and was trying to put out a grease fire with a flammable robe! I was screaming "stop, we have to smother it with a pan or something". By that time, he had pulled the pan of grease off the stove; it splattered up both my legs and onto my robe. My robe proceeded to catch on fire so I pulled it off! Yes, we BOTH are now trying to put out the fire "butt naked", the room has filled with smoke and our son had run out of his room crying and screaming watching his parents "butt naked" trying to fight a fire. I told him to get down and crawl out the front door....and I proceed to ....CAN YOU GUESS...?

You got it, run to the balcony "butt naked" screaming, "help, call the fire department." Seriously.... covering up the important parts...like that mattered. "Help"... "Help"... The sprinklers finally came on after the fire was out.

The fire department finally came as we were running out the door "still naked" fire was out, carpet, kitchen, furniture etc....ruined by fire, smoke or water. So...just when you think you've got it bad...try to remember this story and maybe it will help.

We were determined not to give in or yield. We were knocked down and homeless for a while but we were not out!

There will be times of trial and hysterical laughing at some of it... but how we respond is the key. Respond with faith! Respond with grace and know that you never walk through anything alone.

And....if you can do it with laughter, even better. Laughter is good medicine!

Find JOY in the JOURNEY!

Chapter Questions

1. Do you have an experience were you were unjustly accused or mistreated? How did you respond? Write it down and ask God to show you the places in your heart that still need healing from it.

2. As you look at Job's life think about your foundation. Do you have a strong foundation? What if you were to loose everything, what would you do?

The beauty of God's grace - even in the rain.

3. Do you have any trials that you can look back at and laugh? If so, you are definitely on the right track. Keep lighthearted and try not to let things of this life weigh you down.

4. Share some thoughts on where you are at today. Look at your life and see if there are any cracks in your foundation. Write some down and ask the Lord to help heal those cracks.

13

Sounds of Grace

Their melodic tune awakens my sleep. The continuous song brightens the morning sky and soothes my weary soul. As I listen to the birds, peace rushes over me like a wave. Their songs are graceful and filled with hope.

He sings over me with joy!

I love the songs of the morning, although, I am not a true morning person. I think my internal clock does not officially awaken until 11:00am! As I write, I am in my "happy place" sitting on the balcony of the Lake House. The water is like glass and beckoning me and the breeze is gently blowing across my face. The birds are all in tune and the sun has begun to glimmer across the water. There is something about nature that brings me closer to God. I have such a peace and hope when surrounded by its beauty.

His grace fills the air and covers me like a warm blanket. It stirs a song within and I sing of His amazing grace.

Grace given on the cross, grace covers me when lost, grace that comforts and cleanses sin, grace that brings hope to start again. Grace in the troubles, grace through the pain, grace in the sun and even in the rain.

Grace, Grace, God's great grace.
He gives it freely as we seek His face.

Let the message of Christ dwell among you richly as you teach and admonish one another with all wisdom through psalms, hymns, and songs from the Spirit, singing to God with gratitude in your hearts.
Colossians 3:16

Is anyone among you in trouble? Let them pray. Is anyone happy? Let them sing songs of praise.
James 5:13

What sound stirs in your spirit?

I hear the drum beat loud and clear, it draws me in. It's the cry of God's heart for His people. The beat is louder and faster as though it is a heartbeat. God's heart of grace; the drums are singing their song of grace. There are all kinds of sounds and songs that can speak to our heart and draw us in. Hymns and Christian music are great but I have found God and god's grace in many forms of music and sound. He speaks to me in many ways.

So many times I have heard people say that God only speaks through His Word. Well, He does speak through His word and it's our directional compass and nutrition for our spiritual self. Although, I have found that He can use anything, anyone, any music or sound etc…. to speak and resonate in my spirit. I watched Lord of the Rings and in one scene a big demon like creature tries to cross a bridge and one of the main characters slams his staff into the ground and shouts with great authority…"You shall not pass!" I found my self jumping up and screaming at the TV…"Yeah…that's right!" It spoke volumes to me and stirred up my spirit. I walked around

How does God speak to you?

boldly for days telling the enemy.... you shall not pass and win my soul, my family, etc.... It was awesome. I felt invincible.

Have you ever been driving in the car and a song comes on the radio and it brings you to tears and you realize that you have made a mistake and you want a "do over"? I see a commercial and God speaks. His sounds of grace are all around us. His grace is the gentle breeze and howl of the wind. Don't miss out on His sounds of grace. Be aware and always in tune with what is going on around you. God wants to speak to you wherever you are. It's all in the position of your heart. Be open and pliable to God. He will do great things in you.

As I think about sounds, I think about speech and what comes out of our mouth. So many of us walk around letting what I call "crap" in and "crap" out. I know it's not the best of word choice but sometimes it's the only word that fits. Whatever is in your heart will come out of your mouth eventually. So, if you are surrounding yourself with people who talk negatively, curse etc.... then that is what's going to come out of your mouth.

Do not let any unwholesome talk come out of your mouths, but only what is helpful for building others up according to their needs, that it may benefit those who listen.
Ephesians 4:29

But the things that come out of a person's mouth come from the heart, and these defile them.
Matthew 15:18

Keep focused on God and His promises in the midst of darkness.

Turn on the television and what is on the news.... political nonsense, terrorism, racial propaganda etc..... I wonder how many people get trapped by all of this and buy into the negativity? It's judgmental attitudes and assumptions at every turn. Someone is always trying to get everyone stirred up about something and most of the time it's just that person's perception of what's going on around him or her. It's not even truth. It's crazy out there sometimes.

I do not fully understand nor do I want to understand some of it. I try to keep my eyes focused on what God has promised and what He is calling me to do at this time. If we get so caught up in all of this negative and gossip stuff we will be pulled under and not see a way out. This is not the sound of grace.

Whoever does not love does not know God, because God is love.
1 John 4:8

Wouldn't it be great if we turned on the television to hear a news broadcaster say something like: "I understand what you're feeling and I am sorry for your loss but maybe there's another side to this that you do not know. Let's see if we can get all the facts to help solve this issue. People make mistakes and maybe this happened by accident not because of religion, race or gender etc...." Wow, that would be a first. Let's try to help and not stir up dissention.
Sounds of grace!

He longs for you to receive his grace!

GRACE ON FIRE!

What if everything out of our mouths were of hope, encouragement, love and grace. Can you imagine what life would be like here on earth? I know, I am optimistic and probably a bit naive but I would rather see the good in things than only the bad. I want to live in world where I do not have to worry about what my kids are hearing and seeing when I am not around. Is that too much to ask? Just saying…

My heart longs for sounds of grace. When life gets me down I need His sounds of grace. I am thankful for every moment of His grace. God longs for you to receive His grace and to hear it everywhere you go. As you go along your day, listen to every sound, hear every noise and feel God's grace in every moment. He is there always near you…just listen.

Sounds of grace….

Grace on fire!

Chapter Questions

1. Do you have a favorite song? How does it make you feel? Do you hear God's grace in it?

> Sing and make a joyful noise!
>
> Even if you think it is just noise..lol

2. Are you so in tune with God that you hear His grace in everyday sounds? What sounds are you drawn too? (ex: birds, wind, drums etc...)

2. What does God say through these sounds? If you are not sure stop and listen and try to hear with your heart. Write down what you are hearing and feeling.

4. What kinds of things come out of your mouth? Are they negative or positive? What kind of changes can you make to have a more healthy vocabulary?

5. Do you buy into all the negativity that is on television or in the news? Does it consume you? How does it affect your life?

14

The Awakening of Grace

Arise to a new day! The sun is up and the day is calling for action.

There is a treasure within you!

Grace is awakened by its love. God's great love for you has no boundaries or end. It is greater than comprehension and longer than time. He is ready to show you great and mighty things all through His grace.

"Call to me and I will answer you and tell you great and unsearchable things you do not know."
Jeremiah 33:3

There is a treasure within you!

But store up for yourselves treasures in heaven, where moths and vermin do not destroy, and where thieves do not break in and steal. For where your treasure is, there your heart will be also. Matthew 6:20-21

As I ponder these truths, I see God's love in action. He has given me grace in all situations and He has allowed His grace to cover me in my bad choices as well.

I grew up thinking that everyone thought like I did, saw the best in people and never thought of anything bad happening to me. At college, I went to a "Frat Party". At that time the drinking age had just changed to "21". I was not a drinker and very naïve. I was 21 and not interested in alcohol one bit. I arrived to find a "keg" of beer and a "trash can" full of punch. Of course, I thought…"How nice, they made punch for those who do not drink." I thought it was very creative to put punch in a new, lined trashcan. You see where this is going? LOL

I began dancing with a bunch of friends and was very thirsty. There were no water bottles so my friend brought me some punch. It was a bit tart but good. I sat on the couch for about 30 minutes talking to friends while people kept bringing me new glasses of punch. 5-7 cups later, (I do not quiet remember how many I drank) I tried to stand up and almost fell to the floor. I was terrified and began crying because I thought someone had put something in my drink.

I was mortified when I found out that there was alcohol (not just any alcohol but Everclear, it's hard liquor apparently) in it! I do not know how I got home and into my dorm room. It definitely was the by grace of God!

I should have never put myself in that position. I know better now and I do not drink punch from a trashcan! Just saying…. It's funny now but it wasn't at the time. I am learning more and more about grace as I go through this life. I am so thankful for His grace.

If you have never experienced God's grace or recognized it, He wants to awaken it in you. He is so loving that He gives good gifts to His children and if you are not sure…. just ask. God is only a prayer away.

**Help me God!
Hear my heart's cry!**

Prayer does not have to be some philosophical discussion, the use of big theological words etc.... just speak from the heart. I have prayed many times like this:

God, I don't know what to say but I know you hear me. This stinks, I hate this situation....I need help, I can't do this on my own. Here I am again...just standing here waiting. Help! Are you there? Sometimes I can't hear you. Please show me how to love this person.... etc.....

You get the idea. No fancy words, just the heart crying out to my daddy God.

Growing up in a single parent home was tough at times. Mom worked three jobs just to put food on the table; I was responsible for my little brother, housework, laundry, meals etc.... My dad abandoned us when I was in second grade. He never came around. He made promises to us he never kept and lost his pharmaceutical license because he was selling drugs out of his car.

He was an alcoholic and never sent child support to my mom. It was

What we think is abandonment can be God's protection.

God's grace that protected us from a bad lifestyle. Although there were times when we only had 1 can of soup in the pantry, God always provided.

I did not have an earthly father but I had a heavenly father. I never knew the love of my dad but I found the love of my Daddy God. At first, I thought God was going to abandon or reject me like my earthly father. I also thought I was not good enough to have the love of God. I found out very quickly that God's love and grace is not like that. He will never leave us or forsake us…Ever!

His Grace is Sufficient!

The Lord himself goes before you and will be with you; he will never leave you nor forsake you. Do not be afraid; do not be discouraged."
Deuteronomy 31:8

God also taught me that I am worthy because He is worthy. There is nothing I can do to take away His love for me.

Neither height nor depth, nor anything else in all creation, will be able to separate us from the love of God that is in Christ Jesus our Lord. Romans 8:39

But you are a chosen people, a royal priesthood, a holy nation, God's special possession, that you may declare the praises of him who called you out of darkness into his wonderful light. 1 Peter 2:9

God has called me just as He is calling you to know Him for who He truly is. He wants you to arise and shine to become the person He created you to be! He says come as you are…

He's calling out to you!

"Now will I arise," says the Lord. "Now will I be exalted; now will I be lifted up. Isaiah 33:10

"Arise, shine, for your light has come, and the glory of the Lord rises upon you. Isaiah 60:1

I know I have learned I am so much

more than the world says I am. I am still a work in progress but I am determined to be the best I can be all for the glory of God who created me in His image and has called me by name!

Listen to me, you islands; hear this, you distant nations: Before I was born the Lord called me; from my mother's womb he has spoken my name. Isaiah 49:1

Create in me a pure heart, O God, and renew a steadfast spirit within me. Psalm 51:10

Just as sin reigned in death, so also grace might reign through righteousness to bring eternal life through Jesus Christ our Lord. Romans 5:21

I pray that the eyes of your heart may be enlightened in order that you may know the hope to which he has called you, the riches of his glorious inheritance in his holy people. Ephesians 1:18

"He will wipe every tear from their eyes. There will be no more death or mourning or crying or pain, for the old order of things has passed away." Revelation 21:4

Wouldn't it be great if we all took hold of and accepted God's grace; embraced the change it could make in our lives and world? Grace takes courage as well; to extend grace and love to those who have abused you, been judgmental or racist against you etc. This takes strength and grace that only God can give. Can you imagine the unity this would bring in our world. Grace would catch like wildfire, unstoppable grace! We must have a life on purpose, an intentional life, a life on fire.

Grace on Fire!

You Can Do It!

My prayer for you as you have read this book is that you get a glimpse of God's grace. I hope you began to see it and find it in every aspect of your life. I pray that you will extend grace in every situation and this study has helped you see yourself in a different light. I pray you have found hope and healing through God's grace and will continue to grow in your relationship with Him.

                Your life is worth it.
                  Be intentional.
             You deserve God's best.
              God's Amazing Grace!

Live out Loud!
Sherri

Stories of "Real Life" Grace

Life's Mess

Here is one of my blogs that I had to share with you.

As I walked in the house from a few errands the smell hit me! What is that, it smells like a horse barn or dog kennel that has never been cleaned! I began looking around frantically for the culprit. I walked into the room in which the (three) dogs are kenneled and almost lost it.

My son's 80lb German shepherd we are watching while he is deployed got sick. Throw up, loose poo and diaherrea, everywhere! When I say everywhere, I mean, his kennel, the wood floors, the walls, the windowsills and some on the other two kennels. It looked like a war zone! First things first, don't loose your cookies! Right?! I ran to the bathroom, found some VICKS, placed it in my nose, inside a bandana and outside of the bandana., I looked like a deranged bandit an could still smell it! (so gross)

I made a trail of towels from his kennel to the hall and helped him out of the mess. (Bless his heart, I wouldn't want to stay in there, much less sit in all of that for long) Trails of messy dog prints lined the floor to the back door and back in I went!

I cleaned up some with towels and pulled the liner out. Now the fun part...The liner does not fit through the bedroom door, you have to tilt it on its side. Yes, very quickly, I tilted and scrapped the walls, poo and vomit running down the walls to the floor, on my head, and finally made it outside to the back yard. It was the most disgusting thing I have ever experienced! I had to clean it up because the dog could not do it for himself.

Three hours later, 10 towels rinsed outside, dog kennel bleached, three dogs bathed, I'm clean, floors mopped, rugs vacuumed and I sit down to type AND..... the dog begins to vomit on my good rugs in the study and hallway. ARE YOU KIDDING?!!! I'm done..... rugs are now clean and dogs are staying outside for a while.

As I sit to write God quickly impresses on me.... "This is what my life looks like right now!

It's a mess, I'm undone and living on the edge. This is what it must look like to God. How can He stand me much less love me smelling like this? All of my sin, judgments, hurts etc.... Wow, I wanted to run away when I walked in on the dog's mess but I knew I couldn't. Just like God, I cleaned up the mess, washed him off and loved on him, making sure he was ok.

God is a loving God full of Grace and Mercy! He see's us at our weakest, cleans us up and loves us back to health! What does your life look like right now? Do have a mess that only God can clean? Will you let him wash you and love you back to health? He's calling to you right now. It doesn't matter what you have done or how far you have run from him. He loves you like you never left.

Let's pray:
Father, thank you that you love us beyond our mess! Thank you for your grace and mercy and above all your love. Thank you that you love us beyond measure even when we stink. We give our

hearts to you and ask that you take our sin and wash us clean. Thank you father, In Jesus Name. Amen.

You are Loved! Live Out Loud!

Family and a Haunting Past

She was 16 and wore the Scarlet Letter with great shame. One night of weakness turned to pregnancy. Her family's disappointment bruised and wounded her deeply. Terrified, she walked into the abortion clinic and terminated the pregnancy. This would begin a cycle of rejection, abandonment and abuse in her life.

She turned 18 and married a young man who was verbally and physically abusive. He knew how to make her feel loved, wanted and afraid for her life all in one day. Another unwanted pregnancy and another abortion was in her future. Her mother was the constant voice in her head. "You're never…. you can't…you're a liar etc….." Finally she divorced her husband and returned home to verbal abuse and belittling.

As she was driving home one night a car came out of nowhere and blind-sided her. The car spun out of control hitting a pole. She had several surgeries to repair her back, leaving her in severe pain. Over the course of a year she developed a dependency on painkillers. As her body began to build up a tolerance, she added alcohol to the mix to take the edge off of the pain. (Not only the physical but the emotional as well)

As she entered her mid 20's she sought the love of a man, once again, only to find hurt and abuse at every turn. Another marriage that ended in heartbreak and a mother's nagging and cursing that was never ending. She was never "good enough", "strong enough", or "like her sister" to hear her mother tell it.

She tried life on her own and could not keep a job for any long period of time. Therefore, she would loose her apartment and have to move back in with her parents.

Her sister, a "so called, throw the Bible in your face, Christian" only belittled her and shamed her with every conversation or meeting. The accusations were endless and many times, only their opinion and judgments not truth.

Granted, this woman had a past of drugs, alcohol, stealing and lying but there was no excuse for the judgment and verbal torcher that she endured. (Especially from family and in the name of "Christianity")

Now in her 40's, the loss of many jobs, 4 or 5 abortions, no children and not married…she has given her life to Christ, given up the drugs and is trying to make a new life for herself. You would think her family might support this…. NO, they are still judge and jury. They continue to throw her past in her face, tell her that she hasn't changed etc.….

She is still looking for love in all the wrong places, living with an abusive, argumentative, control freak and still trying to hang on to God's truths. She is searching for His love and seeking His face in the midst of this trial.

I question…."why do those who call themselves "Christians" judge and condemn? God has called us to love! Ok, someone we care about needs help. What do we do? We point them to Christ; His word and love them through their choices and situation. How can people experience love and truth when we are always throwing darts at them? It brings condemnation, rejection etc.…

If we really want to help someone we MUST love! We point them to Jesus, and to an outside counselor if needed and stop judging them. Have we never done anything wrong? My grandmother use to say…"Those without sin should not throw rocks in glass houses." I never truly understood this until later in life. No one is without sin. We have all done something wrong in our lives, probably more than once!

I have counseled this woman since she was in her 20's and walked side by side with her through all of this trying to point her to Jesus and His truth about her. It breaks my heart to hear and see some of the things she has walked through.

Grace must be received to extend it. *We expect grace and forgiveness when we do something wrong so, why not live it out loud to others and give it to them?*
Can you imagine a world full of grace givers?

Grace on Fire!

I pray that if you or someone you know is walking through something similar that you will seek good Godly counseling and seek God's truth in all of it. Try not to let the people who are judgmental and ugly ruin and rule your life. Do not give them power over you. Do not let the enemy win. God is the one who fights on your behalf, just ask!

I know that God will see you through anything.

It may not happen instantly and may take awhile but sometimes we have to go the distance and take the journey so we may grow and learn. You are loved!

A Touchy Subject

Please remember it's the love of God that compels us to share all of His truth, including those things that are hard to hear and *grace doesn't replace truth—it reinforces it.*

I read this earlier this year and thought it was very relevant: *"Changing God's truth is not love; it's a slippery slope. The futile attempt being made to conform God's Word to social norms, rather than to conform social norms to His Word, has nothing to do with love—it's all about acceptance and every man "doing what is right in his own eyes." "Will you accept me and my sin?" has always been the battle cry of man fighting God. Pastors and churches that accept sin rather than lovingly challenge it have three things in common: Truth is vague, doctrine is blurred and the fundamentals of the Christian faith are often avoided. This is not moral progression on God's scale, it's spiritual digression." (Author unknown)*

I watched from the sidelines taking it all in. The young energetic, talented boy who stole our hearts now, in his 40's living a life as a gay man. I watched his Christian Father and friends post belligerent and judgmental words across social media about homosexuality. I am amazed at the intense feelings that this fuels.

We never hear such "heated" words and truths outwardly spoken about, lies (yes even in the church), adultery, cheating, stealing, prostitution, pornography that is rampant (yes, even in the church), etc..... If we are addressing sin as sin, then we need to address all sin and the sin in our own lives not just others.

Most of all I would love to see the approach to the gay lifestyle as one of reaching out in love. Spend time talking and building a relationship with all people and then share your thoughts and truth. The saying goes....*"People don't care how much you know until they know how much you care!"*

I understand that all liars, thieves and cheats are not calling out for equal rights in marriage etc.... but we tend to let the sins that don't "offend" us as much slide. But the ones that "offend" or "disgust" us more...hold the spot light and we decimate them publically. This is not building relationships to show love.

All people need to see the love of God first and need to know you more to understand how God's word is relevant and works in your life and then they can see truth without clouded vision.
Do everything in love.

I know this father has built a relationship with his son and loves him deeply. I know this father is hurting as well. I do not truly understand all of it but I do know that the Holy Spirit grieves when we sit in judgment and openly bash someone else. I am sure the son knows where the dad stands on the subject, growing up in a strong Christian home and doesn't need to be slammed openly for his choices.

I have recently become friends with a woman who lived a gay lifestyle for many years. I would love to share her testimony with you.

As she says: Please know that this is a little "detailed". It is not her intention to upset anyone, but feel like part of her story. It is what she felt that led her into the lifestyle she was living. Here is her story in her own words:

"I want to start by giving a little back ground about how I grew up in order to try and help

people understand what led me to the gay lifestyle. My mom and dad divorced when I was five years old. At six, my mom married the man that was to be my first step dad. Shortly after they got married he began sexually abusing me. He like my dad was an alcoholic. This went on for two years when I finally got the courage to tell my mom.

We left him in the middle of the night and moved from Louisiana to Georgia. Shortly after, my mom moved back to Louisiana and sent me to live with my grandparents. I lived with them for two years, and then moved back home with my mom and siblings. In junior high school, I met a girl and started going to her church.

My mom was raised catholic and during my childhood we had visited a few Baptist churches but nothing regularly. It was in my teen years that I really began struggling with same sex attraction. Although I had always had crushes on girls and not boys, it wasn't until my teen years that I began to truly understand that I was feeling "different". After struggling with this for a few years, finally, I went to my youth pastor at the time and talked with him.

Please keep in mind this was 25 years ago, and homosexuality was something that was not really talked about then like it is today. My pastor told me to just keep praying and that I would be "ok". I left there and decided then that I wouldn't talk to anyone else about it. I prayed a lot back then asking God to take those feelings away from me. I realize now that although I was asking Him to take them away, I really didn't want mean it.

At the age of 14 my mom married another man and we moved yet again. At that time, they decided to put my siblings and I into private school. So, they put us in a Christian school and we began going to church there as a family as well.

I continued to pray and ask God to take those feelings away from me. As a kid growing up, my mom put both my sister and I in sports at a very young age. We both grew up as "tomboys" playing softball, basketball and volleyball.

My mom never really showed emotion or weakness and I learned at an early age that tears, emotion and feelings were just a sign of weakness. It was then I decided that being "tough" was the only way to be. You get hurt; you brush yourself off and keep playing. Somebody hurts you; don't let him or her see it. You want to cry, do it when you are by yourself so that others don't see you as weak.

Through my teen years and after high school I continued going to church. I kept playing softball and struggling with homosexual feelings, but not acting on them. At the age of 21 a man that worked for my stepdad sexually assaulted me. I never told my parents because I was afraid of what my stepdad would do to him. Luckily, the guy never came around again. I confided in my best friend at the time, and she helped me through it the best way she could. However, after all of this, I did not set foot in a church or say another prayer for many years.

At the age of 22 I came "out" as a lesbian and embraced my homosexuality. Six months later, I left Baton Rouge and my family and moved to North Alabama. Soon after, I got into a relationship and was with my first partner for 3 years.

My next partner and I were together for 7 years. I had a few other short-term relationships / dating experiences along the way and then settled down with the girl that I was engaged to until last year when I gave my life to Christ.

Ok, how I got to where I am today... About 3 years ago I reconnected with a friend from my first church on Facebook. I remember sending her a private message and explaining to her where I was at in my life and I understood if she did not want to be friends.

She responded that she didn't agree with my lifestyle but she saw me as an old friend and she wanted to get to know me again. The first few months we really didn't talk much. At the end of 201,1 she had to have knee surgery and as an athlete, I had been through several of those and it gave us some common ground to talk. She still says to this day she thinks God had her go through that to open a door of communication for us.

From there we began talking about our families and just "catching up". One day she asked me what brought me to the point that I was at in my life? Nobody had ever asked me that before. That night, I sat down, wrote her a letter and shared my past with her. We began talking/texting almost daily.

She continued to tell me how much God loved me and that she loved me too. She wanted to know more about homosexuality, so we explored the topic together. We read a few books and would discuss them. I know she prayed for me, a lot! For me, the fact that she was trying to understand me meant the most. We both agreed to be very honest with each other.

There were times when I had to tell her things that I knew in my heart would hurt her but I also knew that the honesty had to be there. One of those times was when my partner and I got engaged and were planning to get married. My friend actually got this news through Facebook and I knew that hurt her. I honestly thought that would be the end of our friendship. It of course was not. She later told me that although she was very hurt and disappointed, she was not giving up on God and me. I still have no idea how she did not lose her patience with me!!

On February 3rd last year, which happened to be my birthday, I was sitting in my bed nursing a hang over. I was looking at Facebook and saw where she had posted about a women's retreat her church was having. I remember thinking to myself; I want to go! So, I sent her a text message asking her if I could attend. I am sure she nearly fell out of the chair she was sitting in when she got that text. She told me that she would love for me to come and sent me the information on how to get registered and I signed up.

Not long after that, I booked my flight to Virginia. Oh, yea, and that wasn't the first time I was supposed to go there to see her. I had planned a trip the summer before that and canceled it. She says now she wasn't truly convinced that I was going to show up until I was on my flight and headed that way.

On April 11th I got on that plane and headed to Virginia. Our reunion at the airport was sweet. She gave me the biggest hug and it was as if the almost 20 years of not having seen each other didn't exist. I flew in the day before the retreat was to start so that we could spend some time catching up with each other and I could meet her family.

The next morning we headed out for the retreat. The truth is, in my mind, I was going there to see a friend I hadn't seen in a very long time, and expecting to go to this church retreat, and for all of the ladies there to judge me because of who I was. I would then be able to tell her I was not interested in her God or her religion and I would be on my way back to my life in Alabama. Well, that is the exact opposite of what happened. So many of the ladies there just accepted me. They came up to talk to me, wanted to get to know me.

God dealt with my heart that weekend and on Saturday night I asked Him to come in to my life and take over. Don't get me wrong; this is something that we had discussed at length! I knew making that decision was not just saying some words. I knew making that decision was going to mean an entire life change for me. At the time, I was in a relationship with a woman and I loved her very much.

My best friend and I had owned a gay bar for 7 years and I worked as a bartender while going to school to be a mechanical engineer. I knew making that decision was going to mean that all of those things were going to change for me.

My friend used to tell me that she prayed everyday that I would be miserable in my lifestyle. Truth is, I was very happy in my life at the time. I had a *partner that I loved very much, I owned a business that was doing well, I was making good money, and I was going to school for something that I truly enjoyed.*

God dealt with my heart when He knew I was ready. It was about six months later when I had the epiphany that I never did get to the point where I was miserable in my life, **I got to the point where I was miserable without HIM in my life.**

After the retreat I flew home to Alabama. I knew a LOT of things were about to change in my life and all I could do was trust God was going to take care of the details. The very first thing He spoke to my heart on, the night that I gave my life to Him, was "you have to completely surrender". I had no idea at the time what that meant but as the days and weeks passed, He continued to speak those words to my heart, "completely surrender to me." All I knew to do was to ask Him to help me to do just that, to surrender it ALL to Him.

As I arrived at the airport and was about to be face to face with my girlfriend, I was terribly nervous. As I started down the escalator, our eyes met. We greeted each other with a hug and got my bags. On the drive home, she said to me, "something is different about you". God opened the door for me to be able to tell her what He had done in my life.

Although she was very sad and hurt, I honestly believe that God prepared her heart for what was coming. Things didn't go nearly as badly as I expected them to. The next step was figuring out how to tell my best friend of 15 years and business partner of 7 years that I couldn't be in business with her and try to convince her to let me sell my ownership in the bar.

I set up a time to meet her for dinner. I honestly didn't know what I was going to say. I just began by telling her what God did in my life at the retreat and how He was changing my heart. To my absolute surprise, she told me she loved me and if that was what I wanted for my life, she was ok with it. She then told me she was almost 50 years old and she was getting tired of the bar scene and we should both just sell.

We talked a little about possible buyers and called it a night. I went home and began praying God would bring the right people in to take over. I know that may sound strange and some of you may think it would have been better for me to want to close it, well, I wasn't at that point, and I believe that God knew it.

What He did do was bring two guys into the picture that wanted to buy the bar. Not only did they want to buy it, when my friend and I told them what we wanted to get for it, they didn't even counter offer. They asked us to give them a few days to get the financing together through their bank and a few days later we were signing the closing papers on the sale of the bar.

Within just a few weeks of returning home, everything really was falling into place for me. God was taking care of all of the details. These things did not come easy for me...He continued to remind me daily that I had to completely surrender to Him.

Next came figuring out where I was going to live. Staying in Alabama really wasn't an option for me. All I had ever known or been known as there was that lifestyle. My friend, others and myself were praying that God would show me where I was supposed to go. Moving back to Baton Rouge didn't seem like the best of ideas *either since my younger sister is currently in the homosexual lifestyle or we had a few mutual friends there as well.*

So, we figured Virginia was the best place for me to be at the time. I would have a great support system there and could stay with my friend and her family until I found a job and a place to live. She agreed to fly to Alabama and make the drive to Virginia with me. I packed what would fit in my car, picked her up at the airport and left Alabama at the end of May.

During this time of transition in my life, I really wanted to make a trip home to see my mom before I got too caught up in life in Virginia. I was now going to be more than 1200 miles away from her and thought I should spend a little time with her while I had the chance.

So, after being in Virginia for two weeks, I headed out to Louisiana. When I arrived, my mom told me she had recently been diagnosed with breast cancer. She was preparing to have surgery and begin chemo treatments. I knew then that I was right where I was supposed to be and that through all of the changes, and the sale of the bar, that God was providing for me to be able to stay with my mom and care for her through this process in her life. Mom came through like a champ and is doing great now.

There are a few things I really want people to get out of my "story". The first thing is that God truly can change anyone!! Here is the thing though; He is not going to push Himself on anyone. We have to genuinely want to change! Next, we are all people, and I truly believe that we all just want to be loved and accepted! We do not have to agree with the way someone lives their lives to love them.

I have heard people say this and it is such a true statement, "people don't care what you know until they know that you care"! Love people the way that you would want them to love you. Lastly, I believe that the biggest thing He taught me through all of this is, in order for true change to take place it requires total and complete surrender. If you really want God to change something in your life, you have GOT to give it ALL to Him...you can not hold on to any part of it and expect Him to change you or your situation."

This is a true story and one that shows how relationship and love allowed truth to come in. This woman no longer lives the homosexual lifestyle. Truth was not bashed over her head or screamed at her in judgment. Love came through and truth prevailed. **Imagine grace extended to a world in need!**

Grace on Fire!

Addicted Teen

At the age of 15 he was offered marijuana. Over the course of a few years, he tried to bring it into the home and was caught at every turn. This led to heavier drugs, experimentation etc... He was angry and rebellious most days; kicked out of the house and welcomed home after true repentance and the willingness to try and get his act together.

At the age of 18 he was invited to a RAVE party. God's grace is so good. He put the desire in this boy's heart not to attend this party. That evening one of his closest friends was shot in the head during a "drive by." If the boy had been with his friend he might have been killed as well.

Three weeks later this young man ran sobbing to his mother and as he fell into her arms he cried out "I can't live like this anymore!" That summer he enlisted into the military and has changed his life for the better. If it weren't for God's grace he would not be with us today. The young man is my son.

Unfortunately, my middle son saw the older one experimenting and he tried some things as well his junior year in high school. But....**God's**

Grace is on Fire and can burn continuously in your life through it all! My middle son has left the nest to spread his wings. He is learning to be a responsible adult and succeeding! I am so proud of both boys and their willingness to learn and grow throughout their journey. Now, on to my daughter, she graduates high school this year and is off to college. I am so proud of them all!

I want to share another mother's story with you (in her words)…

"Let me start by saying it's hard to let His grace flow through you until you really understand how much His grace has flowed TO YOU.

I was a teen mom with a mission to prove all the naysayers wrong and portray an image that all was "hunky dory" in our life. (Picture Perfect) My husband and I got married and were on our own before I graduated high school and bought our first house a year later.

Our first child was not as easy to conform into our "hunky dory" facade. I was easily frustrated and began taking my frustration out on him. I was not walking with the Lord and really at this time in my life, had no idea what it meant or looked like although, I had been going to church since I was a little girl." **(Going to church does not make you a Christian just like standing in a garage does not make you a car.)** "I see now what I wanted was a robot but God gave me a child.

The more I tried to mold him into what "I wanted", the more frustrated and angry I became. The words I spoke to him in anger were words a child should never hear, let alone hear from their mother. As he grew, our fights became more frequent and intense.

One day while I was at a women's retreat I heard the Lord tell me "just write", it was so clear I think had someone been there sitting with me they would have heard it as well. I picked up my pen not knowing what I was suppose to write and twenty minutes later my tear filled eyes looked down at a tear stained letter of apology to my oldest son that I shared with him as soon as I got home that day.

When I put pen to paper that day the Lord opened my eyes and broke through my own justifications for my behavior to come face to face with the reality - I was verbally and sometimes even physically abusing my oldest son.

For so long I had built up this wall of justification for doing what I was doing that I couldn't see what I was truly doing to this child of mine. God's grace flowed to me and He opened my eyes to really see and understand. I felt and really knew undeserved favor." (Grace)

"I'd love to say everything finally became "hunky dory" then, but it didn't, not by a long shot. My son began making choices in high school that would lead him down very dark roads. Roads that would really strain our already strained relationship.

There came a time when we could hardly stand the sight of one another and it was then the Lord reminded me of the grace He showered on me; and forgave me of my biggest mistakes.

The Lord then gave me eyes to see my son how He saw him. God asked me to let His grace flow toward my son. I was to show him undeserved favor and love through his darkest time.

My son began making choices in high school that would lead him down very dark roads where he began drinking and smoking weed. After *barely graduating high school he went with some friends to a summer church retreat and came face to face with Jesus. The Holy Spirit really began to work in him and he chose to attend a few semesters at Bible College in Colorado and California.*

The Lord poured His Word into him during Bible College but still when things got tough he would turn back to his old ways of coping with problems through week and alcohol.

This roller coaster went on for a few years until the girl he wanted to marry more than anything broke up with him and that began the spiral nosedive down.

He became extremely depressed and was more often than not – high and was frequently having dreams about his ex-girlfriend. During the worst of it I attended a women's retreat and the speaker was same woman who spoke at the first retreat I mentioned earlier. The morning of the second day I decided to spend time in the Word before the day got started and the Lord guided me to Ezekiel 34 and when I read verse 16 it was as if the words were jumping off the page and I knew the Lord was speaking to me.

Ezekiel 34:16 says "I will search for my lost ones who strayed away, and I will bring them safely home again. I will bandage the injured and strengthen the weak…"

The Lord gave me so much hope for what was going on with my son and the reminder that He is sovereign and capable of miracles. Well, He didn't stop there, I knew no one at this retreat and had told no one of what I was going through but as the speaker walked around the room and prayed for us, she specifically prayed for lost children to return home when she reached me.

That same day the Lord also brought a wonderful lady into my life, she was a beacon of hope for me. She shared her story and what she had gone through with her son. The Lord took it even further that day. My name was drawn for a gift at the retreat but since it took me so long to make it up to the front to collect it, they gave that gift to another lady who happened to be right there in the front and they handed me another one.

I have to be honest and say I was disappointed to watch that first gift go to someone else because it was impeccably wrapped and I'm a gift-wrap junkie and the gift I did receive was just in a plain bag. My, oh my, how my perspective changed when I opened that little plain bag. Inside was an owl necklace and I knew my son's ex-girlfriend absolutely loved owls.

I didn't know what it meant but I knew it was something because with God there are no coincidences, and I knew I was suppose to share all of this with my son. I didn't know when I would see him again because we had to kick him out of the house about a month prior but the Lord is amazing at logistics and my son happened to come by the house that afternoon when I got home. He also happened to ask how my retreat was and I knew that was the opportunity the Lord was giving me to share all that had happened.

So I pulled my son aside and shared it all, Ezekiel 34, the prayer the speaker said, my new friend and the owl necklace. He broke down and began to cry. He told me he hated his life and I asked him "Do you hate it enough to do something about it? To change it?" He didn't really give me an answer but between Ezekiel and the owl necklace, the Lord planted a seed of hope.

I didn't hear much from him after that for the next two weeks and I'm pretty sure he was high the entire time, then one day he called and said words he had never said before. He said, "I need help mom, I have a problem." One thing led to another and a week later he checked himself into a yearlong, live-in Christian recovery program.

This program was a blessing in so many ways and it was free. For the first few months there he continued to dream about the owl girl. Then one night he had a dream. He saw her dating another guy and she was happy. In the dream he told her that he just wanted her to be happy and from the very bottom of his soul, he really meant it and he was able to let her go. The dream stopped after that but a week later she contacted me and long story short she moved from California to Texas and they were married a few months after his time ended at the recovery program.

The roads my son and I both took really strained our relationship and there were times that we could hardly stand the sight of one another and it was then the Lord reminded me of the grace. He showered so much love and grace on me and my biggest mistakes.

The Lord then gave me eyes to see my son how He saw him and then asked me to let His grace flow through me to my son. I was to show him undeserved favor and love through his darkest time.

It was God's grace alone that led us both to repentance and restoration. We know each other's ugliest parts and choose to love despite all of our shortcomings. This has also caused us to love each other more."

This is such a great picture of our Father's love and grace. The ability to see someone else as God sees him or her is truly God's grace. Sometimes we get caught up with what we think someone should be like and forget that we are just as imperfect. Through our wounds and hurts we look at others through our "pain lens".

God must be allowed in to heal us and remove all calluses from our heart and blinders from our eyes so that we can truly see people the way God sees them. We are all far from perfect, living in a very imperfect world.

Imagine a world on fire with our "Father's eyes". Seeing people out of His "love lens" and

not our "pain lens". God extending us grace so that we in turn can extend grace to all of those around us.

Imagine…a Grace-Filled world!

Will you accept the challenge of receiving God's grace and applying God's grace and love in every area of your life and in this world? In every situation, even the hard ones, to every person, even the hard ones, etc.….

This is Grace on Fire!

References

Bible (NIV, Life Application Bible)

Beth Moore Bible Study (Children of the Day)

Notes from Ministry and Seminary Classes taken over 10 years (Healing and Deliverance, Prophesy and the Prophetic, Generational Curses, Breakthrough etc....)

10 years of Ministerial counseling others

Holy Spirit words of knowledge

Life experiences

About the Author

Sherri loves to create. She found her artistic gift of painting in her late 40's and has begun a successful journey as an artist. Today, she owns a graphic design business called Out of the Box Productions and is the primary graphic artist/designer. She also took up professional photography around the same time and has bloomed as a photographer. Sherri loves music and has been singing since the age of two and has performed at Carnegie Hall, lead worship around the U.S. and has recorded several CDs.

Furthermore, she travels and speaks to various groups as God leads through her ministry, Out of the Box Ministries. Sherri was Ordained in 2006 through Vision International University. She knows the call on her life and tries to walk fully in the grace God has given her.

Sherri began writing as a teen and found her poetic voice early, leading her to write poetry throughout college and adulthood. Her first book 'Poetic Art' is a wonderful coffee table book, which includes many of her first art pieces and great poetry that brings encouragement to all who read it.

Sherri's heart is to love people and with God's grace she helps them find freedom and truth through God's love, his word and laughter.

Sherri grew up in Dallas, TX and was raised by a courageous single mom. Life was not always easy but love out weighed the hard times. She is now married to a wonderful man, Jeff, has three awesome children, a fabulous daughter-in-love and they live in Cypress, TX.

God has created something special in all of us and it is Sherri's prayer that all find freedom, love and truth as we walk this journey together called life.

God never promised it would be easy but he promised to never leave us. He is the way, the truth and the light! His love and grace endure forever.

"As you rediscover God's grace or find it for the first time, may you be forever free and feel forever loved!"

Out of the Box Ministries
Sherri Weeks

www.sherriweeks.com
www.sherriweeksphotography.com

Notes

"Faith is taking the first step even when you don't see the whole staircase."

"Darkness cannot drive out darkness; only light can do that. Hate cannot drive out hate; only love can do that."

Martin Luther King, Jr.

www.ingramcontent.com/pod-product-compliance
Lightning Source LLC
Chambersburg PA
CBHW062204080426
42734CB00010B/1790